The Big Book of
QUILTS
— and —
QUILTING

The Big Book of
QUILTS
— and —
QUILTING

Edited by Rosemary Wilkinson

NEW
HOLLAND

First published in 2005 by
New Holland Publishers (UK) Ltd
London • Cape Town • Sydney • Auckland
www.newhollandpublishers.com

Garfield House, 86–88 Edgware Road, London W2 2EA, United Kingdom

80 McKenzie Street, Cape Town 8001, South Africa

14 Aquatic Drive, Frenchs Forest, NSW 2086, Australia

218 Lake Road, Northcote, Auckland, New Zealand

2 4 6 8 10 9 7 5 3 1

Text, photography and illustrations © 2005 New Holland Publishers (UK) Ltd
Quilt designs © Sharon Chambers, Frances de Rees, Nikki Foley, Katharine Guerrier, Claire Higgott, Jean
Hunt, Gail Smith, Gill Turley, Rose Verney, Sarah Wellfair, Rita Whitehorn, Rosemary Wilkinson,
Margaret Wise, Alison Wood, Dorothy Wood
Copyright © 2005 New Holland Publishers (UK) Ltd

ISBN 1 84537 208 5

Editor: Rosemary Wilkinson
Cover design: Sue Rose
Design: Frances de Rees
Photographs: Shona Wood
Illustrations: Carrie Hill
Template diagrams: Kuo Kang Chen

Reproduction by Pica Digital PTE Ltd, Singapore
Printed and bound in Malaysia by
Times Offset (M) Sdn Bhd

NOTE
The measurements for each project are given in imperial and metric.
Use only one set of meaurements – do not interchange them
because they are not direct equivalents.

Contents

Techniques and Tips

The thirty-five patchwork quilts in this collection are designed for beginners and those whose time is limited. Although they use just three shapes, the square, the rectangle and the triangle, they still show an amazing variety of designs, made all the more exciting by a clever choice of fabrics in five main groups of colourways: fresh, vivid, bright, primary and pastel. These shapes are cut quickly using the rotary cutter rather than with a template and they are machine stitched together with chain-piecing wherever possible. The quilt "sandwich" (of backing fabric, wadding and the pieced top) is held together with machine quilting, big stitch hand quilting or with simple ties and buttons. Two methods are used for the binding – one using four strips applied separately to the four sides, producing abutted corners and the other, slightly more complicated, using a continuous binding, mitred at the corners. Simple appliqué is introduced using a heart template and a technique called slashing or chenille is used as an alternative to piecing to produce a highly textured surface for a really cuddly quilt.

MATERIALS

PATCHWORK FABRICS

The easiest fabrics to work with for patchwork are closely woven, 100% cotton. They "cling" together making a stable unit for cutting and stitching, they don't fray too readily and they press well. Quilting shops and suppliers stock a fantastic range in both solid colours and prints, usually in 45 in/115 cm widths and most of the quilts in this book are based on these cottons.

For each of the quilts featured, there are four alternative colourways, showing the many different effects that can be achieved with each pattern. Fabric designers bring out new ranges all the time and a quick and effective way of choosing fabrics for a quilt is to use the different colourways within one design or different designs in the same colours.

BACKING AND BINDING FABRICS

The backing fabric should be the same type and weight as the fabrics used in the patchwork top. It can be a coordinating colour or it can be a strong contrast. You could also be adventurous and piece the backing too, to make a reversible quilt. In either case the colour of the binding needs to work with both the top and the backing fabric design.

WADDING

Various types of wadding are available in cotton, polyester, wool or mixed fibres. They can be bought in pre-cut sizes suitable for cot quilts and different sizes of bed quilts or in specific lengths cut from a bolt. They also come in different weights or "lofts" depending on how padded you want the quilt to be. Lightweight polyester wadding is the most commonly used but some are more suited to hand quilting. Some need to be closely quilted to prevent them from bunching up, others can be quilted up to 8 in/20 cm apart. Follow the manufacturer's instructions if in doubt.

QUANTITIES

The quantities given at the beginning of each project have been calculated to allow for a bit extra – just in case! The various pieces cut for each quilt use the rotary cutting method and, unless otherwise stated, are cut from across the width of the fabric.

A few of the quilts combine cutting down the length of the fabric with cutting across the width. This is to make the most economical use of fabric or to obtain border pieces cut in one piece.

Unless otherwise stated any 1/4 yard/25 cm requirement is the "long" quarter – the full width of the fabric – and not the "fat" quarter which is a piece 18 x 22 in/50 x 56 cm.

PREPARATION

All fabrics should be washed prior to use in order to wash out any excess dye and to avoid fabrics shrinking at different rates. Wash each fabric separately and rinse – repeatedly if necessary – until the water is clear of any colour run. (If washing in a machine, cut a piece of white fabric from a larger piece. Place one piece in with the wash. After the wash, compare the white fabric with its other half. If they are the same, the fabric did not run. If a particular fabric continues to colour the water no matter how many times it is washed/rinsed and you have your heart set on using it, try washing it together with a small piece of each of the fabrics you intend to use with it. If these fabrics retain their original colour i.e. they match the pieces not washed with the offending fabric, you would probably be safe in using it. But if in doubt – don't!

Once washed and before they are completely dry, iron the fabrics and fold them selvage to selvage – as they were originally on the bolt – in preparation for cutting. Be sure to fold them straight so that the selvages line up evenly, even if the cut edges are not parallel (this will be fixed later).

THREADS

For machine quilting use lightweight or monofilament threads. For quilting by hand, use a thread labelled "quilting thread" which is heavier than normal sewing thread. There are several manufacturers of this thread and it comes in many different colours. Some threads are 100% cotton, others have a polyester core that is wrapped with cotton. You can use a thread either to match or to contrast with the fabric that is being quilted. It is also acceptable to use several colours on the same piece of work. If the quilt is to be tied rather than quilted, use a heavier thread, such as coton perlé, coton à broder or stranded embroidery cotton.

EQUIPMENT

There are some essential pieces of equipment that have revolutionised the making of patchwork. Rotary cutting equipment, consisting of a rotary cutter used with an acrylic ruler and self-healing cutting mat, has speeded up the process of cutting shapes and made it more accurate; the sewing machine makes assembling the patchwork and quilting the finished piece quick and easy.

SEWING MACHINES

The first sewing machine for the home was patented in 1851 and the electric version was made in 1889, although it wasn't in general use until the 1920s when electricity in the home was more widespread. Ever more sophisticated, computerized machines are now available but even a machine with just a straight stitch will speed up the process of assembling and quilting the patchwork considerably. Most sewing machines have a swing needle which allows the zig-zag stitching used for securing appliqué patches. Machines with decorative stitches give the opportunity to make interesting quilting patterns as in the wave pattern used for the "Candy Bars" quilt.

LONGARM QUILTING MACHINES

These are relatively new machines used by professional quilters. You can choose from a huge library of quilting designs. There is also the option to have edge-to-edge quilting, all-over quilting of one design over the entire quilt, or a combination of patterns to complement each other, e.g. medallions, feathers, cables and cross-hatching. Alternatively, you can specify your own freehand style.

One of the advantages of this machine is that the quilt sandwich does not need to be tacked or pinned together prior to quilting: the pieced top, wadding and backing are mounted onto separate rollers which are part of the frame of the machine.

The machine is hand operated and takes considerable skill to operate successfully. Most of the quilters who offer these services advertise in patchwork magazines.

ROTARY CUTTING

Rotary cutting has become the most commonly used method of cutting fabrics for patchwork.

Rotary Cutters

There are several different makes available, mainly in three different sizes: small, medium and large. The medium size (45 mm) is probably the one most widely used and perhaps the easiest to control. The smallest can be difficult to use with rulers. The largest is very useful when cutting through several layers of fabric but can take some practice to use. The rotary blade is extremely sharp, so be sure to observe the safety instructions given opposite. But it does become blunted with frequent use, which makes cutting both hazardous and ineffective, so be sure to have replacement blades available for a large patchwork project.

Rulers

Various different rulers are available for use with rotary cutters. These are made of acrylic and are sufficiently thick to act as a guide for the rotary blade. You must use these rulers with the rotary cutter. Do not use metal rulers, as they will severely damage the blades.

The rulers are marked with measurements and angled lines used as a guide when cutting the fabrics. Ideally these markings should be on the underside of the ruler, laser printed and easy to read. Angles should be marked in both directions. Different makes of rulers can have the lines printed in different colours. Choose one that you find easy on your eyes. Some makes also have a non-slip surface on the back – a very helpful addition.

To start, the two most useful basic rulers are either a 24 x 6 in/ 60 x 15 cm or one that is slightly shorter and the small bias square ruler, 6½ in or 15 cm. This ruler is particularly useful for marking squares containing two triangles – the half-square triangle units. There are many other rulers designed for specific jobs that you can purchase if and when needed.

Self-healing Rotary Cutting Mats

These are an essential companion to the rotary cutter and ruler. Do not attempt to cut on any other surface. The mats come in a number of different sizes and several different colours. The smaller ones are useful to take to classes or workshops but for use at home, purchase the largest that you feel you can afford and that suits your own workstation. It is easier and faster to be able to cut long strips in one go, rather than having to move up the fabric half-way through cutting to fit a smaller board. There is usually a grid on one side of the mat, although both sides can be used. The lines on the mat are not always accurate, so get into the habit of using the lines on the ruler rather than the ones on the mat. Most rotary cutting tools are available with either imperial or metric measurements.

ANCILLARY EQUIPMENT

Most other pieces of equipment are those that you will already have in your workbox. Those listed below are essential but there is also a vast array of special tools devised by experienced quiltmakers which have specific uses. They are not needed by the beginner quilter but can really enhance the type of designs you can make once you've been bitten by the bug.

Scissors: Two pairs are needed. One large pair of good quality scissors should be used exclusively for cutting fabric. The second smaller pair is for cutting paper, card or template plastic.

Markers: Quilting designs can either be traced or drawn on the fabric prior to the layering or added after the layering with the aid of stencils or templates. Various marking tools are available: 2H pencils, silver, yellow, white pencils; fade away or washable marking pens. Whatever your choice, test the markers on a scrap of the fabric used in the quilt to ensure that the marks can be removed.

Pins: Good quality, clean, rustproof, straight pins are essential when a pin is required to hold the work in place for piecing. Flat-headed flower pins are useful because they don't add bulk.

Safety pins: Useful for holding the quilt "sandwich" together for quilting, especially for those who prefer to machine quilt or want the speed of not tacking/basting the three layers together. Place the pins at regular intervals all over the surface.

Needles: For hand quilting use "quilting" or "betweens" needles. Most quilters start with a no. 8 or 9 and progress to a no. 10 or 12. For machine stitching, the needles numbered 70/10 or 80/12 are both suitable for piecing and quilting. Some makers have needles that are labelled "quilting". For tying with thicker thread, use a crewel or embroidery needle.

Thimbles: Two thimbles will be required for hand quilting. One thimble is worn on the hand pushing the needle and the other on the hand underneath the quilt "receiving" the needle. There are various types on the market ranging from metal to plastic to leather sheaths for the finger. There are also little patches that stick to the finger to protect it. Whichever type you choose, it is strongly advised that you do use protection for the fingers on both hands.

HOOPS AND FRAMES

These are only needed if you are quilting by hand. They hold a section of the quilt under light tension to help you to achieve an even stitch. There are many types and sizes available ranging from round and oval hoops to standing frames made of plastic pipes and wooden fixed frames.

Hoops are perhaps the easiest for a beginner. The 14 in/35 cm or 16 in/40 cm are best for portability. Many quilters continue to use hoops in preference to standing frames. When the quilt is in the hoop the surface of the quilt should not be taut, as is the case with embroidery. If you place the quilt top with its hoop on a table you should be able to push the fabric in the centre of the hoop with your finger and touch the table beneath. Without this "give" you will not be able to "rock" the needle for the quilting stitch. Do not leave the quilt in a hoop when you are not working on it, as the hoop will distort the fabrics.

SAFETY

All rotary cutters have some form of safety mechanism which should always be used. Close the safety cover over the blade after every cut you make, whether or not you intend to continue with another cut. Safety habits are essential and will help prevent accidents. Ensure that the cutters are safely stored out of the reach of children.

Keep the cutter clean and free of fluff. An occasional drop of sewing machine oil helps it to rotate smoothly. Avoid running over pins as this ruins the blade. Renew the blade as soon as it becomes blunt, as a blunt blade makes for inaccurate and difficult cutting and can damage the cutting mat. Replacement blades are readily available and there are also blade sharpening/exchange services.

TECHNIQUES

ROTARY CUTTING

The basis of rotary cutting is that fabric is cut first in strips – most commonly across the width of the fabric, then cross-cut into patches. Unless otherwise stated, fabric is used folded selvage to selvage, right sides together, as it has come off the bolt. Before any accurate cutting can be done, the first step is to make sure the edge of the fabric is straight.

MAKING THE EDGE STRAIGHT

1 Place the folded fabric on the cutting mat with the selvages at the top and the bulk of the fabric on the side that is not your cutting hand. Place the ruler on the fabric next to the cut edge aligning the horizontal lines on the ruler with the fold of the fabric and with the selvage.

2 Place your non-cutting hand on the ruler to hold it straight and apply pressure. Keep the hand holding the ruler in line with the hand cutting the fabric. Place the cutter on the mat just below the fabric and up against the ruler. Start cutting by running the cutter upwards and right next to the edge of the ruler (diagram 1).

diagram 1

3 When the cutter becomes level with your extended fingertips, stop cutting but leaving the cutter in position and careful move the hand holding the ruler further along the ruler to keep the applied pressure in the area where the cutting is taking place. Continue cutting and moving the steadying hand as necessary until you have cut completely across the fabric. As soon as the cut is complete, close the safety shield on the cutter. If you run out of cutting mat, you will need to reposition the fabric but this is not ideal as it can bring the fabric out of alignment.

4 Open out the narrow strip of fabric just cut off. Check to make sure that a "valley" or a "hill" has not appeared at the point of the fold on the edge just cut: it should be perfectly straight. If it is not, the fabric was not folded correctly. Fold the fabric again making sure that this time the selvages are exactly aligned. Make another cut to straighten the edge and check again.

CUTTING STRIPS

The next stage is to cut strips to the specified measurement. To do this, change the position of the fabric to the opposite side of the board, then use the measurements on the ruler to cut the strips.

1 Place the fabric on the cutting mat on the side of your cutting hand. Place the ruler on the mat so that it overlaps the fabric. The cut edge of the fabric should be aligned with the vertical line on the ruler that corresponds to the measurement that you wish to cut and the horizontal lines on the ruler should be aligned with the folded edge and the selvage of the fabric.

2 As before place one hand on the ruler to apply pressure while cutting the fabric with the other hand (diagram 2).

diagram 2

CROSS-CUTTING

The strips can now be cut into smaller units, whether squares or rectangles and these units are sometimes sub-cut into triangles.

Squares

1 Place the strip just cut on the cutting mat with the longest edge horizontal to you. Cut off the selvages in the same way as you straightened the fabric edge at the start of the process.

2 Now place the strip on the opposite side of the mat and cut across (cross-cut) the strip using the same measurement on the rule as used for cutting the strip and ensuring that the horizontal lines of the ruler align with the horizontal edge of the fabric. You have now created a number of squares of the required measurement (diagram 3).

diagram 3

Rectangles

1 First cut a strip to one of the required side measurements for the rectangle. Remove the selvages.

2 Turn the strip to the horizontal position as for the squares.

3 Cross-cut this strip using the other side measurement required for the rectangle. Again, ensure that the horizontal lines of the ruler align with the horizontal cut edges of the strip.

Wide strips

Placing two rulers side by side can aid the cutting of extra wide strips. If you don't have two rulers, place the fabric on the cutting mat in the correct position for cutting. Align the cut edge of the fabric with one of the vertical lines running completely across the cutting board and the folded edge with one of the horizontal lines on the mat. If the measurement does not fall on one of the lines on the cutting mat, use the ruler in conjunction with the cutting mat.

Multi-Strip Units

This two-stage method of cutting strips, then cross-cutting into squares or rectangles can also be used to speed up the cutting of multi-strip units to provide strip blocks, such as used for "Rail Fence".

1 Cut the required number and size of strips and stitch together as per the instructions for the block/quilt you are making. Press the seams and check that they are smooth on the right side of the strip unit with no pleats or folds.

2 Place the unit right side up in the horizontal position on the cutting mat. This time when cutting to the required measurement there are more reference points to ensure that you are cutting straight. Align the horizontal lines on the ruler with the cut edges of the strips and with the seam lines just created (diagram 4). If after cutting a few cross-cuts the lines on the ruler do not line up with the cut edges as well as the seam lines, re-cut the end to straighten it before cutting any more units.

diagram 4

ROTARY CUTTING TRIANGLES

Squares can be divided into either two or four triangles and it is the combination of fabrics in these squares and the way they are positioned next to each other which provides many of the fascinating patchwork designs and variations. Both sizes of triangle can be

quickly cut using the rotary cutter or they can be made even faster by a quick piecing method described on page 13.

Cutting Half-square Triangles

1 Cut the fabric into strips of the correct depth and remove the selvages.

2 Cut the strips into squares of the correct width.

3 Align the 45° angle line on the ruler with the sides of the square and place the edge of the ruler so that it goes diagonally across the square from corner to corner. Cut the square on this diagonal creating two half-square triangles (diagram 5).

diagram 5

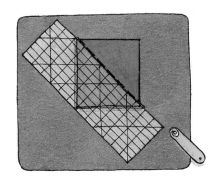

Cutting Quarter-square Triangles

1 Cut the fabric into strips of the correct depth and remove the selvages.

2 Cut the strips into squares of the correct width.

3 Align the 45° angle line on the ruler with the sides of the square and place the edge of the ruler so that it goes diagonally across the square from corner to corner. Cut the square on this diagonal creating two half-square triangles.

4 You can either repeat this procedure on the other diagonal or if you are wary of the fabric slipping now that it is in two pieces, separate the two triangles and cut them individually. Align one of the horizontal lines of the ruler with the long edge of the triangle, the 45° line with the short edge of the triangle and the edge of the ruler placed on the point of the triangle opposite the long edge. Cut this half-square triangle into two quarter-square triangles.

diagram 6

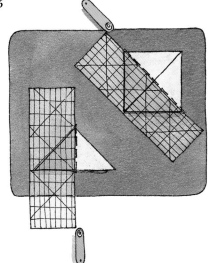

MACHINE STITCHING

NOTES

Seams

Unless otherwise stated, the seam allowances are included in the measurements given and are always ¼ in for imperial and 0.75 cm for metric. The metric seam allowance is slightly bigger than the imperial but it is easy to use in conjunction with the various rotary cutting rulers on the market.

Measurements

The measurements in the quilt instructions are given in both imperial and metric. Use only one set of measurements in any project – do not interchange them because they are not direct equivalents.

To stitch accurately you must be able to use the correct seam allowance without having to mark it on the fabric. To do this you use the foot or the bed of your sewing machine as a guide. Many machines today have a "¼ in" or "patchwork" foot available as an extra. There are also various generic foot accessories available which will fit most machines. Before you start any piecing, check that you can make this seam allowance accurately.

Checking the machine for the correct seam allowance

Unthread the machine. Place a piece of paper under the presser foot, so that the righthand edge of the paper aligns with the right-hand edge of the presser foot. Stitch a seam line on the paper. A row of holes will appear. Remove the paper from the machine and measure the distance from the holes to the edge of the paper. If it is not the correct width try one of the following:

1 If your machine has a number of different needle positions, try moving the needle in the direction required to make the seam allowance accurate. Try the test of stitching a row of holes again.

2 Draw a line on the paper to the correct seam allowance, i.e. ¼ in/0.75 cm from the edge of the paper. Place the paper under the presser foot aligning the drawn line with the needle. Lower the presser foot to hold the paper securely and, to double check, lower the needle to ensure that it is directly on top of the drawn line.

Fix a piece of masking tape on the bed of the machine so that the lefthand edge of the tape lines up with the righthand edge of the paper. This can also be done with magnetic strips available on the market to be used as seam guides. But do take advice on using these if your machine is computerized or electronic.

Stitching ¼ in/0.75 cm seams

When stitching pieces together, line the edge of the fabric up with the righthand edge of the presser foot or with the lefthand edge of the tape or the magnetic strip on the bed of your machine, if you have used this method.

Checking the fabric for the correct seam allowance

As so much of the success of a patchwork depends on accuracy of cutting and seaming, it is worth double checking on the fabric that you are stitching a ¼ in/0.75 cm seam.

Cut three strips of fabric 1½ in/4 cm wide. Stitch these together. Press the seams away from the centre strip. Measure the centre strip. It should measure exactly 1 in/2.5 cm wide. If not, reposition the needle/tape and try again.

Stitch length

The stitch length used is normally 12 stitches to the inch or 5 stitches to the centimetre. If the pieces being stitched together are to be cross-cut into smaller units, it is advisable to slightly shorten the stitch, which will mean the seam is less likely to unravel. It is also good practice to start each new project with a new needle in a clean machine – free of fluff around the bobbin housing.

QUICK MACHINE PIECING

Experienced quilters have devised all sorts of ingenious ways of stitching pieces together to speed up the process of making the components of the blocks. The three most basic techniques used here are for stitching pairs of patches together, for stitching half-square triangle units and for stitching quarter-square triangle units.

Chain piecing

Have all the pairs of patches or strips together ready in a pile. Place the first two patches or strips in the machine, right sides together and stitch them together. Just before reaching the end, stop stitching and pick up the next two patches or strips. Place them on the bed of the machine, so that they just touch the patches under the needle. Stitch off one set and onto the next. Repeat this process until all the pairs are stitched to create a "chain" of pieced patches/strips (diagram 7). Cut the thread between each unit to

diagram 7

separate them. Open out and press the seams according to the instructions given with each project.

Stitching Half-square Triangle Units

This is a quick method of creating a bi-coloured square without cutting the triangles first.

1 Cut two squares of different coloured fabrics to the correct measurement, i.e. the finished size of the bi-coloured square plus $\frac{7}{8}$ in/2.5 cm. Place them right sides together aligning all raw edges. On the wrong side of the top square draw a diagonal line from one corner to the other.

2 Stitch $\frac{1}{4}$ in/0.75 cm away on either side of the drawn line.

3 Cut the two halves apart by cutting on the drawn line. Open out and press the seams according to the instructions given with each project (diagram 8). You now have two squares each containing two triangles.

Stitching Quarter-square Triangle Units

This method also creates triangles from squares without first cutting the triangles.

1 Cut squares to the finished size of a square containing four triangles plus $1\frac{1}{4}$ in/3.5 cm. Follow the stitching, cutting apart and pressing sequence as for the half-square triangles units.

2 Place the two bi-coloured squares right sides together. Ensure that each triangle is not facing a triangle of the same colour. Draw a line diagonally from corner to corner, at right angles to the stitched seam.

3 Pin carefully to match the seams, then stitch $\frac{1}{4}$ in/0.75 cm away on either side of this drawn line. Before cutting apart open up each side and check to see that the points match in the centre. Cut apart on the drawn line. You now have two squares each containing four triangles (diagram 9).

diagram 8

diagram 9

PRESSING

Each individual project will have instructions on the direction in which to press the seam allowances. These have been designed to facilitate easier piecing at junctions and to reduce the bulk so that seam allowances do not lay one on top of the other. Pressing as you complete each stage of the piecing will also improve the accuracy and look of your work. Take care not to distort the patches. Be gentle, not fierce, with the iron.

ASSEMBLING THE QUILT

Most patchwork tops are framed by one or more borders. The simplest method of adding borders is to add strips first to the top and bottom of the quilt and then to the sides, producing abutted corners. A more complicated method is to add strips to adjacent sides and join them with seams at 45 degrees, giving mitred borders. Only the first method is used for the quilts in this book.

ADDING BORDERS WITH ABUTTED CORNERS

The measurements for the borders required for each quilt in the book will be given in the instructions. It is, however, always wise to measure your own work to determine the actual measurement.

1 Measure the quilt through the centre across the width edge to edge. Cut the strips for the top and bottom borders to this length by the width required for the border.

2 Pin the strips to the quilt by pinning first at each end, then in the middle, then evenly spaced along the edge. By pinning in this manner it is possible to ensure that the quilt "fits" the border. Stitch the border strips into position on the top and bottom edge of the quilt (diagram 10). Press the seams towards the border.

diagram 10

3 Measure the quilt through the centre top to bottom. Cut the side border strips to this measurement.

4 Pin and stitch the borders to the each side of the quilt as before (diagram 11). Press the seams towards the border.

diagram 11

QUILTING

The three layers or "sandwich" of the backing/wadding/pieced top are held together by quilting or by tying. The quilting can either be done by hand or machine. The tying is done by hand by stitching decorative ties at strategic points of the quilt. Buttons can also be used for the same purpose.

Layering/Sandwiching

Prior to any quilting, unless you are using a longarm quilting machine (see page 8), the pieced top must be layered with the wadding and the backing. The wadding and the backing should be slightly larger than the quilt top – approximately 2 in/5 cm on all sides. If the quilt edges are to be finished with a binding the three layers are assembled in the order that they will appear in the finished quilt, i.e. backing at the bottom, wadding in the middle and patchwork on top. If there is no binding, the sequence before stitching together is: backing fabric, patchwork, then wadding.

Assembling prior to binding

1 Lay out the backing fabric wrong side uppermost. Ensure that it is stretched out and smooth. Secure the edges with masking tape placed at intervals along the edges to help to hold it in position.
2 Place the wadding on top of the backing fabric. If you need to join two pieces of wadding first, do so by butting the edges and stitching together by hand using a herringbone stitch (diagram 12).

diagram 12

3 Place the pieced top right side up and centred on top of the wadding.

Assembling where no binding is used

1 Spread out the wadding on a flat surface. Smooth out to ensure there are no wrinkles.
2 Place the backing fabric centrally on top of the wadding right side uppermost.
3 Place the pieced top centrally over the backing, wrong side uppermost. Pin with straight pins around the edges to keep them together.
4 Stitch around all four sides with a $\frac{1}{4}$ in/0.75 cm seam allowance but leaving an opening of about 15–18 in/35–45 cm in one of the sides.

5 Trim away excess wadding across the corners to reduce bulk, then turn the quilt right side out, so that the wadding is now in the middle and slip-stitch the opening closed.
6 Smooth out the layers of the quilt and roll and finger-press the edges so that the seam lies along the edge or just underneath.

Basting prior to quilting

If the piece is to be quilted rather than tied, the three layers now need to be held together at regular intervals. This can be done by basting or by using safety pins. For either method, start in the centre of the quilt and work out to the edges.

Using a long length of thread start basting in the centre of the quilt top. Only pull about half of the thread through as you start stitching. Once you have reached the edge, go back and thread the other end of the thread and baste to the opposite edge. Repeat this process stitching in a grid over the whole quilt top (diagram 13).

diagram 13

MACHINE QUILTING

Designs to be used for machine quilting should ideally be those that have one continuous line. The lines can be straight or free form curves and squiggles. For either type be sure to keep the density of stitching the same. With either method continuous lines of stitching will be visible both on the top and on the back of the quilt. It is a quick method but requires careful preparation.

There is a wide variety of tools available designed to help make handling the quilt easier during the machine quilting process. But the most essential requirement is practice.

It is worth making up a practice sandwich – if possible using the same fabrics and wadding as used in the actual quilt – to be sure that you get the effect you want. In any case, plan the quilting design first, otherwise there is a danger that you will start with quite dense stitching, then tire of the process and begin to space out the lines producing an uneven pattern.

When starting and stopping the stitching during machine quilting, either reduce the stitch length to zero or stitch several stitches in one spot. If you do not like the build-up of stitches that this method produces, leave long tails on the thread when you start and stop. Later pull these threads through to one side of the quilt, knot them, then thread them into a needle. Push the needle into the fabric and into the wadding but not through to the other side of the quilt and then back out through the fabric again about 1 in/2.5 cm away from where the needle entered the quilt. Cut off the excess thread.

Straight Line Machine Quilting

One of the easiest and most common forms of straight line quilting, is called "in-the-ditch" and involves stitching just beside a seam line on the side without the seam allowances. Some machines require a walking foot to stitch the three layers together. These are used with the feed dogs up and, while in use, the machine controls the direction and stitch length.

Free Motion Machine Quilting

When machine quilting in freehand, a darning foot is used with the feed dogs down, so that you can move the quilt forwards, backwards and sideways. This is easier on some machines than others but all require a bit of practice.

Hand Quilting

The stitch used for hand quilting is a running stitch. The needle goes into the quilt through to the back and returns to the top of the quilt all in one movement. The aim is to have the size of the stitches and spaces between them the same.

1 Thread a needle with an 18 in/45 cm length of quilting thread and knot the end. Push the needle into the fabric and into the wadding but not through to the back about 1 in/2.5 cm away from where you want to start stitching. Bring the needle up through the fabric at the point where you will begin stitching. Gently pull on the thread to "pop" the knot through into the wadding.

2 To make a perfect quilting stitch the needle needs to enter the fabric perpendicular to the quilt top. Holding the needle between your first finger and thumb, push the needle into the fabric until it hits the thimble on the finger of the hand underneath.

3 The needle can now be held between the thimble on your sewing hand and the thimble on the finger underneath. Release your thumb and first finger hold on the needle. Place your thumb on the quilt top just in front of the position where the needle will come back up to the top and gently press down on the quilt top (diagram 14).

diagram 14

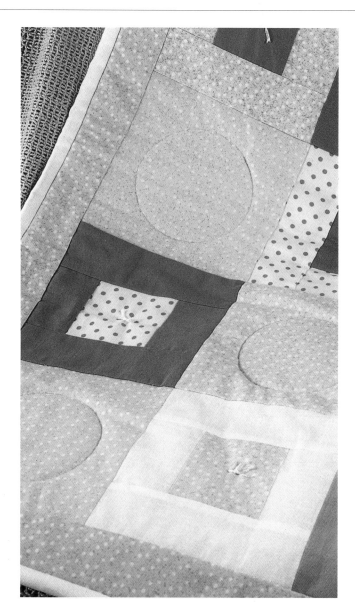

4 At the same time rock the thread end of the needle back down towards the quilt top and push the needle up from underneath so that the point appears on the top of the quilt. You can either pull the needle through now making only one stitch or rock the needle up to the vertical again, push the needle into the quilt top, then rock the needle back down to the quilt top again placing another stitch on the needle. Repeat until you can no longer rock the needle into a completely upright position (diagram 15). Pull the needle through the quilt. One stitch at a time or several placed on the needle at

diagram 15

once – "the rocking stitch" – before pulling the thread through, are both acceptable.

5 When the stitching is complete, tie a knot in the thread close to the quilt surface. Push the needle into the quilt top and the wadding next to the knot but not through to the back of the quilt. Bring the needle up again about 1 in/2.5 cm away and gently tug on the thread to "pop" the knot through the fabric and into the wadding. Cut the thread.

Big Stitch Quilting

For these super quick quilts, another form of hand quilting, known as "Big Stitch" is used, which speeds up the process of quilting by hand and adds another design element. "Big Stitch" uses coton perlé no. 8 as the thread and a larger needle with a bigger eye. The stitches are also larger and the quilting designs simpler. The quilting stitch for the "Big Stitch" is also a running stitch.

BINDING

Once the quilting is completed the quilt is usually (but not always) finished off with a binding to enclose the raw edges. This binding can be cut on the straight or on the bias. Either way the binding is usually best done with a double fold. It can be applied in four separate pieces to each of the four sides or the binding strips can be joined together and stitched to the quilt in one continuous strip with mitred corners. To join straight-cut pieces for a continuous strip, use straight seams; to join bias-cut pieces, use diagonal seams (diagram 16).

diagram 16

For either method the width of the bias strips should be cut to the following measurement: finished binding width x four + the seam allowance x two.

For example:

A finished binding width of $\frac{1}{2}$ in would be cut as $2\frac{1}{2}$ in:

$(\frac{1}{2}$ in x 4$) + (\frac{1}{4}$ in x 2$) = 2\frac{1}{2}$ in

or 1.25 cm would be cut 6.5 cm:

$(1.25$ cm x 4$) + (0.75$ cm x 2$) = 6.5$ cm

Binding the four sides separately

1 Cut binding strips to the required width. Fold in half lengthwise with wrong sides together and lightly press.

2 Measure the quilt through the centre from top to bottom and cut two of the binding strips to this length.

3 Pin one of the strips down the side of the quilt, right sides together and aligning raw edges. Stitch with the usual seam allowance.

4 Fold the binding strip to the back of the quilt and slip stitch to the backing fabric. Trim the ends level with the wadding. Do the same on the opposite side of the quilt with the other strip.

5 Measure the quilt through the centre from side to side and add 1½ in/4 cm for turnings. Cut two more binding strips to this length, joining if necessary. Stitch to the top and bottom of the quilt, turning in a short hem at either end before folding to the back and slip-stitching down. Slip stitch the corners neatly.

Continuous strip binding

1 Fold the binding in half lengthwise with wrong sides together and lightly press.

2 Place the binding's raw edges to the raw edge of the quilt – somewhere along one side, not at a corner. Commence stitching about 1 in/2.5 cm from the end of the binding and, using ¼ in/0.75 cm seam allowance, stitch the binding to the quilt through all layers of the "sandwich" stopping ¼ in/0.75 cm from the end. At this point backstitch to secure, then break off the threads. Remove the quilt from the sewing machine.

3 Place the quilt on a flat surface with the binding just stitched at the top edge, fold the binding strip up and away from the quilt to "twelve o'clock", creating a 45° fold at the corner (diagram 17).

diagram 17

4 Fold the binding back down to "six o'clock" aligning the raw edges of the binding to the raw edge of the quilt. The fold created on the binding at the top should be the same distance away from the seam as the width of the finished binding. i.e. ½ in/1.25 cm from seam line to fold (diagram 18).

diagram 18

5 Start stitching the binding to the quilt at the same point the previous stitching stopped, ¼ in/0.75 cm from the edge of the quilt top. Secure with backstitching, then continue to the next corner. Repeat the process at each corner.

6 Stop about 2 in/5 cm from where you started. Open out the fold on both ends of the binding, then seam the two ends together. Trim away the excess, refold and finish applying the binding to the quilt.

7 Trim the excess wadding and backing fabric so that the distance from the stitching line equals or is slightly wider than that of the finished binding. Fold the binding over to the back and hand stitch the folded edge of the binding to the quilt along the row of machine stitching just created. A mitre will appear at the corners on the front and on the back of the binding. Slipstitch these in place (diagram 19).

diagram 19

HANGING SLEEVE

If your quilt is a wallhanging or is to be exhibited it will need a hanging sleeve. A sleeve can be added after the quilt is completely finished but a more secure and permanent sleeve can be added along with the binding. Stitch the binding to the front of the quilt and before folding it over onto the back add the sleeve.

1 Cut a piece of fabric, preferably matching the backing, to measure 10 in/25 cm by the width of the quilt. Make a 1 in/2.5 cm hem on both the short ends.

2 Fold the fabric in half along the length with wrong sides together. Centre this on the back of the quilt aligning the raw edges of the sleeve with the raw edges of the quilt. Secure with pins (diagram 20).

diagram 20

3 Turn the quilt over so the front is uppermost. Taking care to remove the pins as you approach them, stitch the sleeve to the quilt by stitching along the row of stitching made when applying the binding.

4 Finish hand stitching on the binding.

5 Lay the quilt on a flat surface with the back uppermost. Gently roll the top layer of the tube up to the top edge of the binding so it forms a fold along this edge. Secure with pins. Now smooth out the rest of the sleeve tube until it rests evenly on the back of the quilt (diagram 21).

diagram 21

6 Stitch the sleeve to the back of the quilt along the fold at the bottom of the sleeve and at each end so that when a rod is inserted it will not actually touch the back of the quilt only the sleeve fabric. Take care that your stitches only go into the back and wadding of the quilt and are not visible on the front. Remove the pins. The sleeve is now stitched to the quilt and has a slight bulge in it. This bulge will allow room for a rod to go through the sleeve without distorting the quilt when it is hung.

LABELLING

Your quilt should be signed, dated and placed. This information provides a record for your own information as well as for those in the future.

The details can be incorporated on the quilt front or on a label attached to the back. This label can be simply handwritten with a permanent pen or made very elaborate with pieced, embroidered or fabric painting. Another way of making an individual label is with the help of modern technology: the computer and the colour printer.

TIPS

Strip cutting

To cut strips longer than the length of the ruler, fold the strip in half and cut half the length. To cut strips wider than the width of the ruler, either use two rulers side by side or use the markings on the cutting mat plus the ruler but this is not quite so accurate.

Chain piecing

To further speed up this process place the two pieces/strips to be stitched together beside the sewing machine. Place one group of patches facing up and one group facing down. Now when you pick up one piece its partner is in the correct position to place on top right sides together.

Pressing seams

Always press seams to one side unless otherwise stated, as an open seam is put under more strain. Press fabrics towards the darker fabric to prevent show-through.

Slip-stitched seams

For quilts that are made by the bagging out method, i.e. without a binding, to finish the slip-stitched seam neatly, before you turn your quilt, stitch across the turning opening using the longest stitch your machine will make. Finger-press the seam allowance open quite firmly. Now rip out the long stitches, turn the quilt and you will find you have an obvious straight crease line to follow when hand stitching.

Measuring borders

Even if measurements are given for border strips, it is always worth double-checking against your own pieced top. Measure through the middle of the quilt, as the edges can become stretched.

Attaching borders

Once you have determined the size of the top, bottom and side borders, fit the pieced top to these measurements rather than the other way round. Mark the centre and quarter points of the borders and of the quilt sides and match up. You may need to ease the sides of the quilt to fit the borders, but this will help to give a flat square quilt rather than one with wavy borders.

Storage

Store quilts in an old pillowcase or acid-free tissue paper rather than in a plastic bag, which doesn't allow fabrics to breathe and therefore encourages mould.

Shadow Work

Designed by Dorothy Wood

Shadow work is a technique normally stitched on a small scale for cushions or wallhangings but it works equally well on a quilt. The quilt top fabric is decorated with bright coloured squares of fabric, fixed in place with fusible webbing. A layer of fine muslin is laid on top and the quilt sandwich is quilted by hand to keep the wonderful soft feel of the muslin. This single bed quilt is made entirely by hand but because the stitches can be fairly large and there is no piecing, it only takes a few days to make.

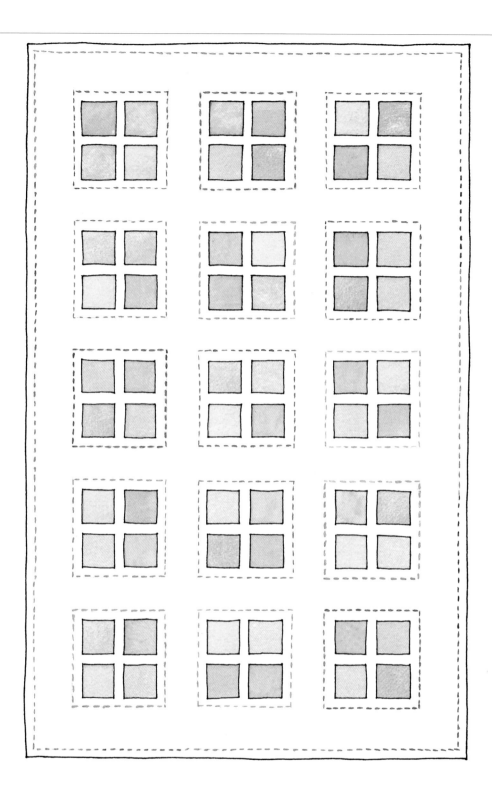

NOTE Choose deep coloured fabrics for this quilt, as they will pale significantly with the layer of fine muslin on top and make sure they are colourfast.

Finished size: 57½ x 89¼ in/146 x 226 cm

MATERIALS
All white fabrics used in this quilt are 59 in/150 cm wide. Coloured fabrics are 45 in/115 cm wide

Coloured squares: lime, deep pink, coral, turquoise, purple and fuchsia cotton fabric, 10 in/25 cm of each
Fusible webbing: 18 x 59 in /45.5 cm x 1.5 m
Baking parchment

Fine white muslin: 2¾ yds/2.40 m
White cotton: 2¾ yds/2.40 m
Backing: white, 2¾ yds/2.40 m
Wadding: 2 oz polyester, 60 x 96 in/152 x 243 cm
Quilting frame: 14 in/36 cm
White sewing thread
Tapestry needle
Stranded embroidery cotton: lime, deep pink, coral, turquoise, purple and fuchsia to match coloured squares

ALTERNATIVE COLOUR SCHEMES

1 This bold tie dye print produces a wonderful broken pattern on the quilt. Choose a fabric with plenty of white so that the splashed paint pattern is distinct. 2 Using a white fabric with large, brightly coloured spots creates an unusual effect as the spots seem to float in the quilt. 3 Checks work well so long as the design is simple and the background colour light enough so that the squares show quite clearly through the muslin. 4 The plain black fabric with deep grey stitching gives a simple Japanese look to the quilt and would be ideal in a boy's bedroom.

1

2

3

4

CUTTING

1 From each of the coloured fabrics cut ten
4¾ in/12 cm squares. Place the squares side by side on
the fusible webbing. Cover with baking parchment
and iron with a medium hot iron. Peel off the backing
paper and separate the squares using a rotary cutter.

ASSEMBLING

1 Fold the white cotton fabric in half lengthwise and
crosswise and crease along the folds. Lay out flat.
Place four different fabric squares, fusible webbing
side down, in the centre leaving a ¾ in/2 cm gap
between each (diagram 1). Check that they are
absolutely straight, cover with baking parchment and
press with a medium iron to secure.

diagram 1

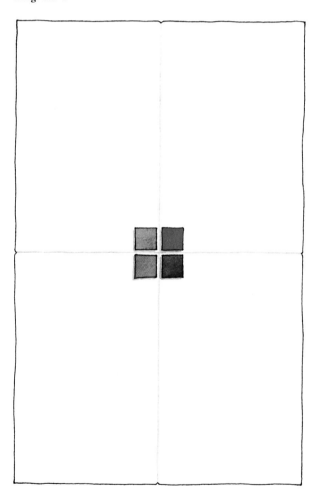

2 Measure out 6 in/15 cm to one side of the top
right square and position the first (top left) square of
the second block of four. Using a different combination of colours, position the next three squares with
the same gaps between. Check they are straight and
press to secure.

3 Continue spacing the blocks of four squares
6 in/15cm apart until there are three blocks across
the width and five lengthwise as shown in the quilt
assembly plan on page 22. Press the backing fabric
and lay flat. Place the wadding on top, then cover
with the quilt top. Finally place the fine muslin on
top. Pin through the layers, inserting two pins in each
coloured square.

STITCHING

1 Lay the quilt flat. Fit a quilting frame around the
first block of squares and quilt around the edge of
each square using white sewing thread. The stitches
do not have to be tiny, 4 to 5 to the inch/2.5 cm is
ideal. Move the frame from block to block and quilt
around every square with white thread.

2 Using the tapestry needle and a quilter's rule as a
guide, score a line around one of the blocks
1 in/2.5 cm away from the coloured squares. Choose
a colour of stranded embroidery cotton to match one
of the squares. Quilt along the scored line using a single strand of cotton (diagram 2). Repeat the process
on each block changing the colour each time.

diagram 2

3 Lay the quilt flat. Score a line 6 in/15 cm away
from the coloured blocks all the way around the
edge. Quilt with stranded cotton, changing the colour
each time you start a new thread.

FINISHING

1 Fold back the muslin along the outside quilted line down one side. Fold the backing fabric underneath along the same line. Score a line on the white quilt top fabric, 1 in/2.5 cm out from the stitching. Trim this fabric and the wadding along this line (diagram 3). Repeat on all four sides.

2 Flatten out the muslin and backing fabric, then trim both, ¾ in/2 cm from the edge of the wadding. Fold the backing fabric over the wadding along one side and turn the muslin under the quilt top fabric. Pin the edges together. Repeat on all four sides.

3 Slipstitch the edges together, taking care to stitch the corners securely (diagram 4).

diagram 3

diagram 4

Round Peg, Square Hole

Designed by Rose Verney

This is an extremely simple design which works well to a small or large scale. I have used thirty-six squares in twelve colours to make this throw. You could change the size either by changing the dimensions of the squares and circles or by altering the number that are cut. The quilt does not have to be made square, it would work equally well as a bed quilt.

Finished size: 48 x 48 in/118 x 118 cm

MATERIALS
Plain fabric: fat quarters of each of 12 colours: I have used two greens, three blues, two yellows, three pinks, orange and apricot
Pair of compasses or 8 in/20 cm diameter plate
Backing: blue cotton, 52 x 52 in/128 x 128 cm

Wadding: 2 oz, 52 x 52 in/128 x 128 cm
Small buttons: 25
Fabric marking pencil
Crochet cotton: white
Fabric marking pencil
Binding: one fat quarter of a thirteenth colour: I have used lilac

ALTERNATIVE COLOUR SCHEMES

1 The palest of pastels makes a fresh and summery quilt made even prettier with white or pale pink stitching. 2 I adore stripes, lots of these are shirtings, again easy to find at jumble sales. Arrange the directions of the stripes differently. 3 A collection of predominantly black prints from my scrap bag makes a bold, dramatic colour scheme. 4 Dark rich colours which are subtle variations on rust, chestnut and olive look great with black stitching.

1

2

3

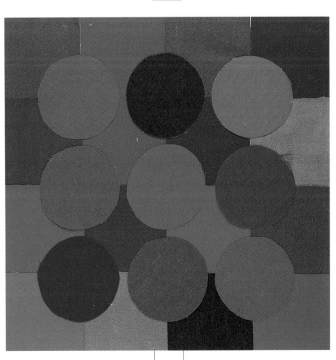

4

CUTTING

1 Cut three 8 in/20 cm squares from each of the 12 plain coloured cottons.

2 Cut nine 8 in/20 cm circles (make a paper circle template with a compass, or use a plate and draw around it) from nine of the 12 plain colours.

3 For the border, using the leftovers of all the colours, cut pieces measuring 2¾ in/7 cm deep and anything from 1 to 6 in/2 to15 cm wide (diagram 1).

diagram 1

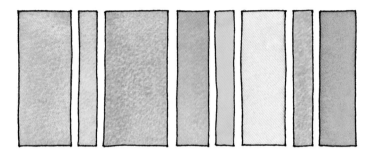

> *NOTE* You can cut lots of these in advance, but I find it easiest to cut and join at the same time – start joining the pieces, then keep cutting and adding more until you have four strips of joined pieces measuring 2¾ x 47¾ in/7 x 118 cm – join them in any order: enjoy trying out different colours next to each other!

STITCHING

1 Pick out six squares each in a different colour and stitch them together in a strip, taking a ¼ in/0.75 cm seam allowance. Press the seams open.

2 Stitch together the remaining six colours in the same way.

3 Do this twice more, using the colours in the same order as steps 1 and 2. (This way you will avoid finding any squares of the same colour falling next to each other.) Press the seams open. Join the six strips as shown in diagram 2. As you will see, the two centre strips are upside down. Press open all the seams.

diagram 2

4 Place the nine circles over the joins following the quilt assembly plan on page 28. Be sure to place the circles in such a way that each of the nine colours falls on four different colours, i.e. not on a square of the same colour - this is quite easy! Pin and baste, keeping the basting stitches at least ½ in/1.5 cm from the raw edges.

5 Turn in ⅛ in/3 mm on each circle and hem, turning in as you go and using the needle to help you achieve a smooth curve. Press again, making sure all the seams on the back are flat.

FINISHING

1 If you haven't already done so, join the pieces for the striped border. When you have four border strips each 47¾ in/118 cm long, press all the seams open and stitch to the pieced top in a log cabin arrangement as shown in the quilt assembly diagram on page 28.

2 Spread the backing right side down on a flat surface, then smooth the wadding and the patchwork top, right side up, on top. Fasten together with safety pins or baste in a grid.

3 Using the white crochet cotton, quilt around the circles, and diagonally over the squares using big stitches. Use a fabric pencil to draw guidelines. Quilt an extra circle inside each big circle, in the centre. (Use a glass or cup to guide you.)

4 Sew on 25 buttons, one at each junction and one in each circle, leaving a tuft of thread to tie into a knot. Trim the ends.

5 Cut the fabric for the binding, 2½ in/6.5 cm wide. Join the binding strips with diagonal seam to make a continuous length to fit all round the quilt and use to bind the edges with a double-fold binding, mitred at the corners.

Apricot Wave

Designed by Rose Verney

The inspiration for this design came from a 1950s print dress my mother wore when I was a child, with a design of squiggles, polka dots and doodly lines. I have used a lovely, subtly textured white/yellow shot cotton as the base and have added two panels of pieced stripes at the sides, using all the colours of the central section plus another pink for good measure.

Finished size: 45½ x 47¼ in/115 x 120 cm

MATERIALS
All fabrics used in the quilt top are 45 in/115 cm
wide, 100% cotton

Central panel: pale yellow shot cotton, 1⅓ yds/1.20 m

Appliqué patches and striped panels: palest pink:
½ yd/50 cm; dark apricot: ½ yd/50 cm; light pink, mid
pink, bright yellow, pinkish tan, apricot: fat quarters of
each of these
Crochet cotton: white
Backing: mid pink, 1⅓ yds/1.20 m
Wadding: lightweight, 49 x 51 in/124 x 129 cm
Binding: dark apricot (included in allowance above)

ALTERNATIVE COLOUR SCHEMES

1 A selection of my favourite greens set against a rich buttercup yellow makes a really sunny colour scheme. 2 A cosy and colourful combination of warm pinks using wonderful shot cottons. 3 A sophisticated monochrome palette from charcoal grey through to a bleached-out green/grey, again in shot cottons. 4 Based on natural calico, these colours have a fresh, seaside feel.

1

2

3

4

CUTTING

1 Cut the central panel from the yellow fabric, 47¼ x 24¼ in/120 x 62 cm.

2 Make templates using the diagrams on pages 38 and 39 enlarged to full size. Cut the appliqué shapes from the templates, following the arrows for the direction of the grain of the fabric. There are eleven lines of appliqué and I have used five different fabrics, twice, and the dark apricot for the centre line of "U" shapes.

3 Cut thick and thin strips randomly from all colours for the two side panels, except the dark apricot, each 11 in/28 cm long. The thin stripes vary between 1 and 1¾ in/2.5 and 4.5 cm and the thick stripes from 2 to 3½ in/5 to 8.5 cm, including seam allowance. You will need approximately 17 wide strips and about the same number of narrow strips for each panel, depending on the widths. Vary the widths slightly and mix the colours as you like.

STITCHING

1 Pin the appliqué shapes to the central panel, centering them between the two sides of the panel and spacing the rows evenly, following the quilt assembly plan on page 34. Baste all the shapes on, keeping your stitches at least ⅜ in/1 cm from the raw edge.

NOTE The "S" shapes need to be positioned so that they overlap slightly, then when they have been hemmed they will be the right space apart. The spaces between the shapes should be similar but don't have to be exact.

2 Turn under about ⅛ in/2 to 3 mm and hem around the edges. Turn the edge in as you stitch, using your needle to help make smooth curves (diagram 1). Press, leaving the basting thread in place.

diagram 1

3 Using the white crochet cotton, work running stitch around the edge of each shape, about ⅛ in/ 3 mm from the hemmed edge. Press again and remove basting stitches.

4 Stitch the thick and thin stripes together for the two side panels, using a ¼ in/0.75 cm seam. They should each measure 47¼ in/120 cm long. Press all the seams open, trimming them if necessary to make the work lie flat. Stitch the two side panels to the centre panel, using a ¼ in/0.75 cm seam. Press the seams towards the centre.

FINISHING

1 Spread the backing right side down on a flat surface, then smooth the wadding and the patchwork top, right side up, on top. Fasten together with safety pins or baste in a grid.

2 Quilt through all layers, using the same thread as for the decorative stitching on the appliqué. Stitch a vertical line down each side of the central panel and ad lib horizontally (diagram 2).

diagram 2

3 For the binding, cut strips of dark apricot fabric 1½ in/4 cm wide, either straight or bias cut and join to make a continuous length to fit all round the quilt, then use to bind the edges with a single-fold binding, mitred at the corners.

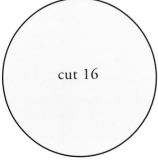

cut 16

All templates are 70% of full size. Enlarge on a photocopier.

Arrows show straight grain of fabric. Snip all inner curves and corners as indicated. Approximately ⅛ in/3 mm has been allowed for hems.

Jouy Medallion Wallhanging

Designed by Rosemary Wilkinson

Toile de Jouy fabric with its different cameos of idyllic country life is chosen as the centrepiece of this medallion quilt. The measurements given are based on the diamond cut from the largest of these cameos – other fabrics may need different measurements, so the quilt is designed with adaptable sizes and piecing patterns.

Finished size: 37 x 37 in/93 x 93 cm

MATERIALS
Feature fabric and backing: 2½ yds/2.20 m pink and white toile de Jouy, 56 in/144 cm wide. The amount is generous to allow for the cutting of the central square.
Checked fabric: red and white, 1 yd/1 m, 56 in/144 cm wide

Red fabric: 32 in/80 cm, 41 in/104 cm wide
Dressmaker's pattern paper: 1 sheet
Middle fabric: 1¼ yds/1 m white lawn, 41 in/104 cm wide
Bamboo pole or wooden dowel rod: 41 in/104 cm long
Two cup hooks

ALTERNATIVE COLOUR SCHEMES

Choose the feature fabric first, then pick out two complementary fabrics. 1 This cat and mouse novelty print makes a fun design for a child's bedroom. 2 Choose the brightest colours from the botanical motifs to keep this design lively. 3 Mix and match muted florals to make a calm design perfect for a bedroom. 4 Plates taken from a novelty print matched with a lively check produce a crisp design.

1

2

3

4

CUTTING

1 Find the best motif on the toile de Jouy. Find the vertical centre, fold and lightly press. Find the horizontal centre, fold and lightly press. Open out, then measure an equal distance from the centre in each direction, so that you are showing all of the motif, and mark. For the piece shown, I measured 8 in/22 cm. Using a ruler, align the marks and cut out the diamond shape. The sides of the square measure 12½ in/31 cm.
Reserve the remainder for the triangles and the backing.

2 From the checked fabric, cut a strip across the width, 3 in/7.5 cm deep, then cross-cut into four rectangles, 12½ x 3 in/31 x 7.5 cm;
cut 6 strips across the width, 1 in/2.5 cm deep;
cut 16 squares, 3 in/7.5 cm, for the pinwheels.

3 From the red fabric, cut a rectangle, 12 x 3 in/ 30 x 7.5 cm, then cross-cut into four squares;
cut 6 strips across the width, 1½ in/4 cm deep;
cut 3 strips across the width, 1 in/2.5 cm deep;
cut 16 squares, 3 in/7.5 cm, for the pinwheels;
cut 4 strips across the width, 1½ in/4 cm deep for the binding;
cut 1 strip across the width, 5 in/12.5 cm deep for the tabs.

STITCHING

1 Stitch one red 3 in/7.5 cm square to each end of one of the checked 12½ in/31 cm rectangles. Repeat. Press the seams towards the corner squares.

2 Stitch one of the checked 12½ in/31 cm rectangles to one side of the centre toile de Jouy square. Stitch another to the opposite side of the square.

3 Stitch one of the strips made in step one to the third side of the square and repeat with the remaining strip. Press the seams away from the centre square.

4 Place the pattern paper underneath the square, so that one side rests along a diagonal. Work out where the apex of a right-angled trangle will be and mark (diagram 1). Measure one side and add 1¼ in/3.5 cm. Cut two squares from toile de Jouy to this measurement, then sub-cut both on the diagonal.

diagram 1

5 Stitch one triangle to one side of the central square and a second to the opposite side. Press the seams towards the striped fabric.

6 Stitch the remaining two triangles to the opposite sides and press as before.

7 Take the 6 red strips, 1½ in/4 cm deep, the 6 checked strips, 1 in/2.5 cm deep and the 3 narrower red strips, 1 in/2.5 cm deep. Stitch together along the long sides in the sequence shown in diagram 2. You will have three five-bar strips.

diagram 2

8 Stitch eight pinwheels using the 3 in/7.5 cm squares of red and checked fabric and following the method in step 2 of adding the borders to the Sawtooth Stars quilt on page 63. Trim the pinwheel sides to fit the depth of the five-bar strips.

9 Stitch one pinwheel to one end of one of the five-bar strips. Press the seam away from the pinwheel. Match the centre of the pinwheel to the centre of one edge of the central square, mark the edge of the square on the five-bar strip, add a ¼ in/0.75 cm allowance and cut the strip (diagram 3).

diagram 3

10 Stitch the five-bar strip to the other side of the pinwheel, press, match to the central square, add the seam allowance and cut as before.

11 Stitch a pinwheel to either end of these two strips. Press the seams away from the pinwheels. Repeat to form another strip of three pinwheels.

12 Repeat steps 9 and 10 but don't add the seam allowance. Stitch these strips to the top and bottom of the central square. Stitch the remaining two strips to the sides of the central square.

ADDING THE BORDERS

1 Cut 6 strips, 1½ in/4 cm deep, across the width of the checked fabric. Repeat on the toile de Jouy. You may not get full strips from the toile de Jouy, depending on how it was cut for the central medallion.

2 Place one strip of checked fabric with one of toile de Jouy, right sides together and stitch down one long edge, taking the usual seam allowance. Repeat with the remaining strips, then cross-cut these strips into 4¼ in/11 cm rectangles.

3 Measure the pieced top through the centre from side to side, then add 8½ in/22 cm to this measurement. Stitch the rectangles together along the longer sides, alternating fabrics to make four strips to the measured length. Slightly adjust the seams between the strips if necessary to make the exact measured length.

4 Stitch the borders to the pieced top and mitre the corners.

FINISHING

1 Cut a piece 1¼ yds/1 m square from the toile de Jouy for the backing and from the white lawn.

2 Spread the backing right side down on a flat surface. Smooth the white fabric and the pieced top, right side up, on top. Fasten together with safety pins or baste in a grid.

3 Machine quilt "in-the-ditch" round the central medallion, on either side of the five-bar strips and diagonally across the pinwheels.

4 Join the binding strips into one length long enough to go all round the quilt and use to bind the quilt with a double-fold binding, mitred at the corners.

5 Fold the 5 in/12.5 cm strip for the tabs in half along the length, right sides together. Stitch down the long side taking the usual seam allowance, then turn right side out and press with the seam in the middle.

6 Cross-cut into five 4½ in/11.5 cm pieces. Fold in half with the seam on the outside. Stitch across the short end. Turn inside out and press. Lay evenly across the top of the wallhanging and stitch in place.

7 Thread onto the bamboo pole and hang from cup hooks.

Flower Strippy

Designed by Frances de Rees

Placing striped patterns next to traditional florals emphasizes the strip design of this easily pieced quilt. Ten different prints are used here, so this quilt could be a good excuse to finally use up some of those scrap fabrics, although you do need a full width of each. The strips are cut with a rotary cutter, quickly machine-pieced and simply hand-quilted using the strips as a guide.

Finished size: 61½ x 45½ in/156 x 116 cm

MATERIALS
All fabrics in the quilt top are 45 in/ 115 cm wide 100% cotton

Large strips: prints **a**, **c** and **e**, 9 in/23 cm of each; prints **f**, **i** and **j**, 4½ in/11.50 cm of each

Small strips: prints **b** and **g**, 7½ in/19.50 cm of each; prints **d** and **h**, 5 in/13 cm of each
Binding: an extra 8 in/20 cm of one of the strip fabrics: I used print **h**
Border: an extra 15 in/40 cm of one of the strip fabrics: I used print **c**
Backing: 3½ yds/3.25 m
Wadding: 64½ x 49½ in/166 x 126 cm
Quilting thread: ivory

ALTERNATIVE COLOUR SCHEMES

1 Using darker hues of the same colour frames the lighter shades and shows them to their best advantage. 2 The subtle effect of using similar red tones gives this a warm abstract feel. 3 The vertical stripes included here draw the eye to the picture panels. 4 The clash of patterns is effective because of the similarity of tone and colour shades.

1

2

3

4

CUTTING

1 From prints **a**, **c** and **e**, cut 2 strips across the width of the fabric, 4½ in/11.5 cm deep.

2 From prints **f**, **i** and **j**, cut 1 strip across the width of the fabric, 4½ in/11.5 cm deep.

3 From prints **b** and **g**, 3 strips across the width of the fabric, 2½ in/6.5 cm deep.

4 From prints **d** and **h**, 2 strips across the width of the fabric, 2½ in/6.5 cm deep.

5 From the border fabric, cut 5 strips across the width, 2¾ in/7 cm deep.

6 From the binding fabric, cut 5 strips across the width, 3½ in/9 cm deep.

NOTE   It may help to pin scraps of the off-cuts in the correct sequence as shown in diagram 1 on a piece of paper. This is useful reference to avoid adding a strip in the wrong order.

STITCHING

1 Put to one side two **a** strips and two **b** strips. Arrange the remaining strips in order of assembly as shown in diagram 1. Stitch the strips together along the width of the fabric taking a ¼ in/0.75 cm seam allowance. Press all the seams in the same direction.

diagram 1

2 Using a rotary cutter and ruler, trim the edges of the panel to level them. Fold the stitched panel in half widthwise and measure across the width at the top. Divide this measurement into three, then cut the panel lengthwise into three equal panels (diagram 2).

diagram 2

3 Turn the central panel upside down, then replace between the two side panels. Stitch the three panels together, taking the usual seam allowance and aligning all horizontal seams where appropriate (diagram 3). The horizontal seams are now lying in opposite directions and this helps the seams lie flatter. Do not

diagram 3

press the seams open as this would weaken the seams and also seams pressed to one side make it easier to quilt "in-the-ditch" at a later stage.

4 Add one strip **b** to the top and one strip **b** to the bottom of this pieced panel. Repeat with the two **a** strips. Trim the edges level with the rest of the panel.

ADDING THE BORDERS

1 Measure the pieced panel through the centre from side to side, then trim the two shorter border strips to this measurement. Stitch to the top and bottom of the panel.

2 Join the remaining three border strips into one length. Measure the pieced top through the centre from top to bottom, then cut two strips to this measurement from the joined piece. Stitch to the sides of the panel (diagram 4).

diagram 4

FINISHING

1 Cut the wadding and backing fabric 3 in/7.5 cm larger than the quilt top on all sides. Spread the backing right side down on a flat surface, then smooth the wadding and the pieced top, right side up, on top. Fasten together with safety pins or baste in a grid.

2 Quilt "in-the-ditch" along all seams either by hand or machine.

3 Join the binding strips to fit the long sides of the quilt. Fold in half and press. Pin one strip to the side of the quilt, aligning raw edges. Stitch, then fold over to the back of the quilt and slip stitch in place. Repeat with the second side, then do the same for the top and bottom of the quilt.

Eight Pointed Stars

Designed by Katharine Guerrier

Eight pointed star blocks are made in a range of patterned pastels set into crisp white sashing strips with corner posts. Some of the star blocks are made with extra detail in the centres providing interest and variety and linking the fabrics used in the stars. A vibrant pink is used for the binding. The quilting is done on a "Gammil" long arm machine by Beryl Cadman of "Custom Quilting Limited".

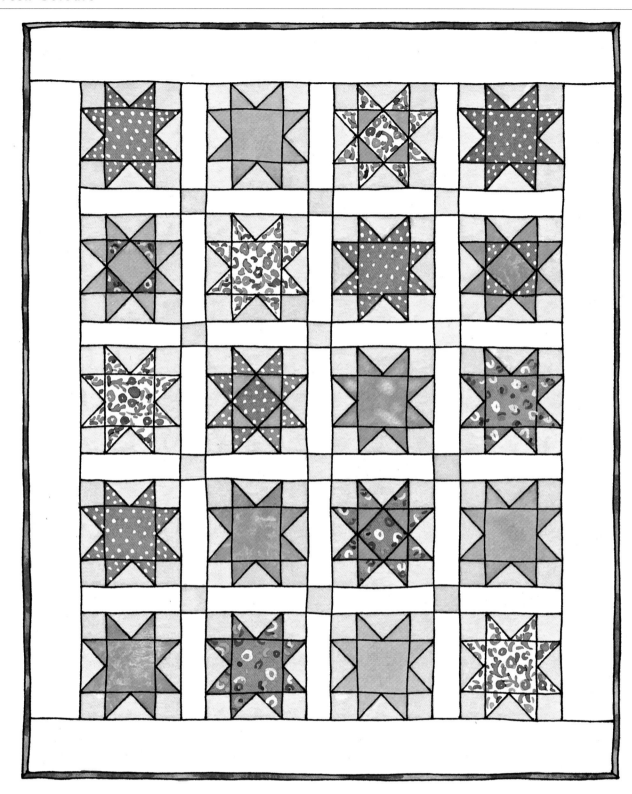

Finished size: 48 x 58 in/122 x 147 cm

MATERIALS

All fabrics in the quilt top are 45 in/115 cm wide 100% cotton

Star fabrics: three pink and two green fat quarters in a range of patterns: spots, floral or marbled

Background to the stars and corner posts: yellow, 1¼ yds/1 m

Sashing, backing and borders: white, 3¾ yds/ 3½ m

Binding: magenta pink, ½ yd/50 cm

Wadding: 54 x 64 in/137 x 163 cm

Quilting thread: pastel variegated thread

ALTERNATIVE COLOUR SCHEMES

1 The contrast in this block between the star fabric and the background is created by the difference in scale of the prints. 2 For maximum visual impact, team black with a highly contrasting bright colour. 3 Use solid colours to emphasize the geometric shapes in the block for a good graphic effect. 4 There is a wide range of batik fabrics in subtle colours available to quiltmakers which will give your blocks a contemporary appeal.

1

2

3

4

CUTTING

1 From the star fabrics, cut one 4½ in/11.5 cm square for the centre; cut eight 2½ in/6 cm squares for the star points. This is enough for one block, you will need 20 sets in total.

2 From the yellow background, cut four 2½ in/6 cm squares for the corners; cut four 4½ x 2½ in/11.5 x 6 cm rectangles for the star points. This is enough for one block, you will need 20 sets in total.

3 For the 'Diamond in a Square' detail on some block centres, in addition to the 4½ in/11.5 cm squares just cut, cut four 2½ in/6 cm squares in one of the other star fabrics. You will need 5 sets in total.

4 Before cutting out the sashing strips, from the white fabric, cut four strips for the borders, 5¼ in/ 13.5 cm wide and 49 in/124.5 cm long, and make up the backing piece 56 x 66 in/142 x 168 cm.

5 From the remaining white sashing fabric, cut 31 strips, 8½ x 2½ in/22 x 6 cm.

6 From the remaining yellow fabric, cut twelve 2½ in/6 cm squares for the corner posts.

7 From the magenta pink, cut strips of binding, 2½ in/6 cm deep to a total length of 215 in/547 cm.

STITCHING

To make one star block:

1 Place one of the 2½ in/6 cm squares of star fabric over a yellow 2½ x 4½ in/ 6 x 11.5 cm rectangle, aligning the lefthand side and with right sides together. Draw a diagonal line as shown in diagram 1 and stitch on this line. Cut the corners away ¼ in/0.75 cm from the stitching line.

diagram 1

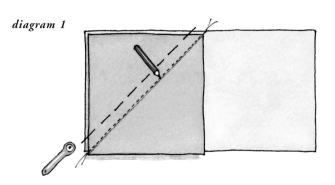

2 Open out and press the seam towards the triangle.

3 Place a second 2½ in/6 cm square of star fabric over the rectangle, aligning the righthand side, draw a diagonal line and stitch as before.

4 Trim and press as before. Repeat three more times to make four star point units altogether (diagram 2).

diagram 2

5 To make the centre detail (on five blocks only), place two of the 2½ in/6 cm squares, which you have cut from one of the other star fabrics, at opposite sides of the centre square, right sides together and aligning corners, draw two diagonal lines as shown in diagram 3 and stitch along these lines. Cut away the corners ¼ in/ 0.75 cm from the stitching.

diagram 3

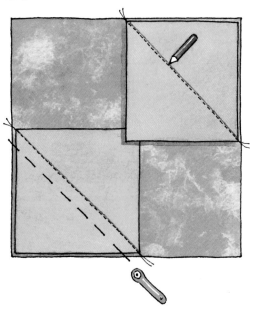

6 Open out and press the seams towards the triangles.

7 Repeat on the remaining opposite sides of the centre square with the other two matching 2½ in/6 cm squares. Open out and press as before (diagram 4).

diagram 4

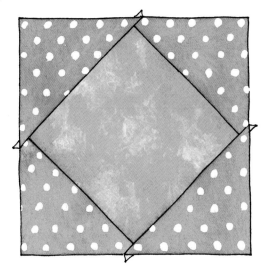

8 Stitch the blocks together as illustrated in diagrams 5a and 5b, matching points where necessary. Make four blocks in each of the five star fabrics adding the centre detail to one in each set (twenty blocks altogether, five with centre detail).

diagram 5a

diagram 5b

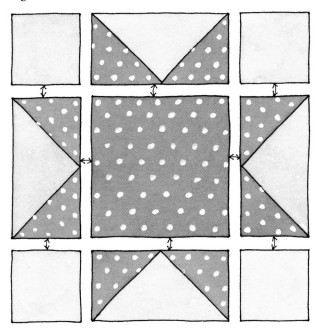

9 Lay out the blocks on a flat surface, following the quilt assembly plan on page 54.

10 Stitch four columns of five blocks together with a white sashing strip between each block.

11 Stitch the short sides of five sashing strips with a yellow corner post between each. Repeat twice to make three sets of sashing strips and corner posts.

12 Stitch the four columns of blocks together with a set of sashing strips between each column.

13 Stitch border strips to the two longer sides of the quilt, press the seams, then stitch the remaining two border strips to the top and bottom of the quilt.

FINISHING

1 Spread the backing right side down on a flat surface, then smooth the wadding and the pieced top, right side up, on top. Fasten together with safety pins or baste in a grid.

2 Quilt by hand or machine in the desired quilting pattern. The quilt photographed was quilted on a long arm machine in edge-to-edge "hearts and daisies" pattern using pastel variegated thread.

3 Join the binding strips and use to bind the quilt with a double-fold binding, mitred at the corners.

Sawtooth Stars

Designed by Maggie Wise

This vibrant little quilt is very easy and quick to make using a rotary cutter and quick piecing techniques. You could literally piece it in one weekend and quilt it in another.

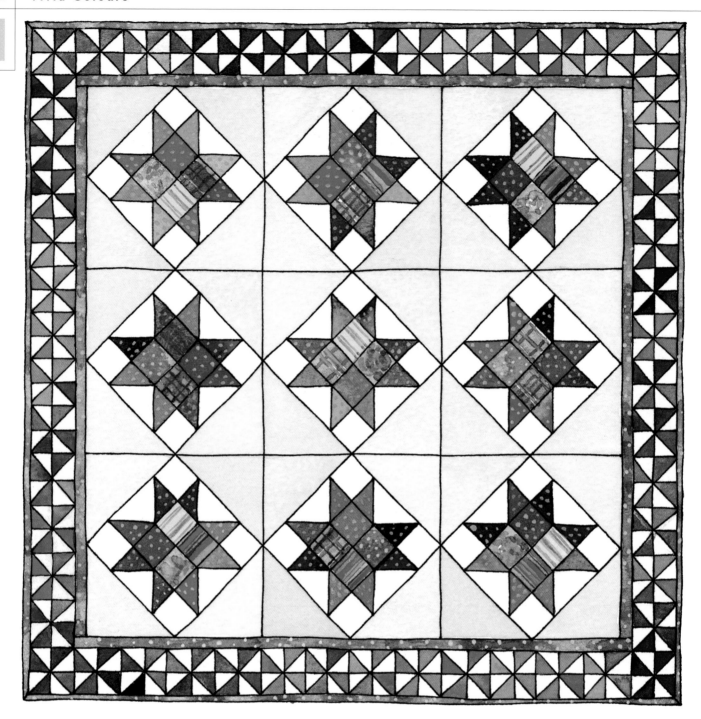

Finished size: 72 x 72 in/183 x 183 cm

MATERIALS
All fabrics used in the quilt top are 45 in/115 cm
wide, 100% cotton

Star backgrounds and pinwheel borders: white,
2 yds/1.70 m
Star points and pinwheel borders: multi-coloured
fabric, 1⅜ yds/1.40 m

Star centres: 8 bright prints, 6 in/15 cm of each
colour
Star setting triangles: 4 very pale prints, 24 in/60 cm
of each
Inner border and binding: green spot fabric,
1¼ yds/1.10 m
Backing: very pale print, 75½ x 75½ in/192 x 192 cm
Wadding: 2 oz polyester, 75½ x 75½ in/192 x 192 cm

ALTERNATIVE COLOUR SCHEMES

This quilt is made up of a number of fabrics in a general range of colours with the pinwheels and stars establishing the tone. The background colour is also important for setting off these other fabrics. The alternative schemes below show how you can achieve different moods for the quilt. 1 Homespun: using muted checks and small florals. 2 Provençal: crisp flowery fabrics. 3: Sweet liberty: using soft cotton lawn fabrics. 4 Forest green: a strong collection of leaf designs and bold greens.

CUTTING

1 For the star blocks, cut:

36 x 6½ by 3½ in/16.5 x 9 cm rectangles from white for star points (**a**);

72 x 3½ in/9 cm squares from multi-coloured fabric for star points (**b**);

36 x 3½ in/9 cm squares from eight bright prints for block centres, (**d**);

36 x 3½ in/9 cm squares from white for corners (**e**);

20 x 10 in/25.5 cm squares from four pale prints (cut 5 squares from each colour); sub-cut each square once diagonally to make the setting triangles.

2 For the inner border, from green spot fabric cut 2 strips across the width and 2 in/5 cm deep. Piece together along the short edges, then cut:

2 strips, 51½ x 2 in/133 x 5 cm for the top and bottom;

2 strips, 54½ x 2 in/141 x 5 cm for the sides.

3 For the outer pinwheel borders, cut:

104 x 3⅛ in/8 cm squares from multi-coloured fabric;

104 x 3⅛ in/8 cm squares from white.

NOTE

If you place the two fabrics right sides together and press before you cut the squares for the pinwheels, they will be ready for marking and stitching.

4 For the binding: cut 8 x 2 in/5 cm strips.

STITCHING

1 To make the four-patch centres, place two bright print squares (**d**), right sides together and stitch, taking a ¼ in/0.75 cm seam allowance. Press the seam towards the darker fabric. Repeat with two more squares.

2 Stitch the two-square units together matching the centre seam carefully. (The way they are pressed will help them to nestle nicely.) This makes the centre of the block (diagram 1). Repeat to make a total of nine.

diagram 1

3 To make the star point units (**c**), take one white piece (**a**) and two multi-coloured pieces (**b**). Mark each piece (**b**) with a diagonal line from corner to corner. Place one piece (**b**) on one piece (**a**), right sides together, aligned to one end (diagram 2).

diagram 2

4 Stitch diagonally along the marked line, then trim back the corner to a ¼ in/0.75 cm seam. Open out and press the seam towards the darker fabric.

5 Repeat on the opposite end of (**a**) using the second piece (**b**). This makes unit **c** and you will need to make four of these units for each star (36 in total).

6 To make the Sawtooth Star block, take four (**c**) units, one four-patch centre and four (**e**) pieces. Assemble the star in strip units as shown in diagram 3. Repeat to make a total of nine.

diagram 3

7 Take two setting triangles in different colours. These are cut oversize, then trimmed to give perfect sized blocks. Stitch one to each side of the centre block using a ¼ in/0.75 cm seam allowance. Press the seams away from the centre.

8 Take two more setting triangles, again in different colours and stitch one to each of the remaining sides of the star block. Press the seams away from the centre.

9 The next stage is trimming. Line up the side of the centre square with the 45 degree line on your ruler. Ensure a generous ¼ in/0.75 cm allowance projects beyond the star block and trim (diagram 4).

diagram 4

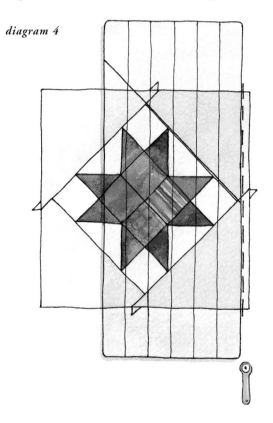

10 Join the blocks into three rows of three blocks as shown in the quilt assembly plan on page 60. Stitch the blocks into rows, then stitch the rows together. This makes the centre section.

ADDING THE BORDERS

1 Stitch the top and bottom inner borders to the centre section, followed by the side inner borders as shown in the assembly plan. Trim level if necessary.

2 To make the pinwheel borders, take the 104 pairs of 3⅛ in/8 cm squares. Mark each pair diagonally, then stitch ¼ in/0.75 cm each side of the line. Cut on the marked line to make two half-square triangles. Piece these together to make pinwheel blocks (diagram 5).

diagram 5

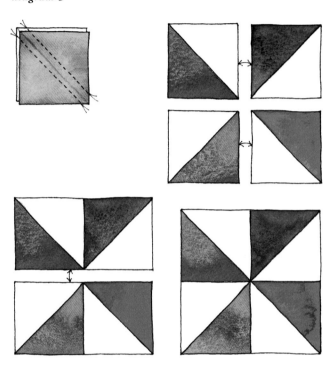

3 For the top and bottom borders stitch 12 pinwheel blocks together and join to the quilt. For the side borders use 14 blocks.

FINISHING

1 Give the backing and the pieced top a good press, then spread the backing right side down on a flat surface. Smooth the wadding and the pieced top, right side up, on top. Fasten together with safety pins or baste in a grid.

2 I did not need to mark the quilt. I quilted it free-hand by machine, in rows to form a water-like pattern. I wanted an all-over, but tranquil pattern that emphasized the watery coloured fabrics I'd used to set the stars. I used a medium sized vermicelli pattern to emphasize the movement in the pinwheel border.

3 Join the binding strips into one length long enough to go all round the quilt and use to bind the quilt with a double-fold binding, mitred at the corners.

Glow Worms

Designed by Claire Higgott

The background for this quilt is quickly and easily made with free cut blocks, so there is very little measuring involved! The blocks have been arranged so that the colours shade from dark to light across the quilt but they would also look good used randomly. The spirals (or glow worms!) bring the quilt to life and are bonded in place before stitching.

Quilt size: 50 x 66 in/122.5 x 161.5 cm

MATERIALS

All fabrics used in the quilt top are 45 in/115 cm wide.

Batik fabrics for the blocks, borders and binding: nine different blue shades, ½ yd/50 cm of each

Batik fabrics for the spirals: orange and green, 6 fat quarters in total or a variety of scraps (at least 9 in/ 23 cm square for the large spirals and 6 in/15 in square for the small spirals)

Fusible webbing: 1½ yds/1.50 m

"Stitch and Tear": 1 yd/1 m

Backing: navy blue print, 56 x 72 in/137.5 x 176.5 cm

Wadding: lightweight, 56 x 72 in/137.5 x 176.5 cm

ALTERNATIVE COLOUR SCHEMES

1 Spots and stripes can swim before your eyes and cause all sorts of optical illusions but here the neutral colours temper the effect and would suit a modern setting. 2 The blue floral fabrics, which are very similar in value, make a subtle background for the deep blue spirals. 3 The combination of black and white is always striking and the scarlet spiral stands out graphically against the background. 4 Bright orange prints give this colourway a real zing.

1

2

3

4

CUTTING
(Cut strips selvage to selvage unless otherwise indicated.)

1 From each of the nine blue fabrics, cut a 5 in/ 12.5 cm strip for the borders and a 2 in/5 cm strip for the binding and set these aside.

2 Divide the rest of each of the blue fabrics into four equal pieces – they should measure 10 to 11 in/ 25.5 to 28 cm square but this is not crucial! There should be thirty-six pieces in total.

STITCHING
(Use a ¼ in/0.75 cm seam allowance throughout.)

1 Sort the thirty-six square-ish pieces into pairs. If you want to shade the background of the quilt, most of the pieces should be paired, so that the values are similar - light with light, medium with medium, dark with dark. However a few "crossover" pairs – light with medium and medium with dark – will help the shading process. Alternatively, you could pair the fabrics randomly.

2 Arrange each pair one on top of the other with right sides uppermost and press together.

3 Take one of the pairs and place it on the cutting board. If they are fairly square it doesn't matter which way round they go. However, if one side is longer than the other make sure the longer side is closest to you. Using a rotary cutter and ruler – but without measuring – make four cuts through the two fabrics as shown by the dotted lines in diagram 1. The exact position and angle of the cuts will vary with each pair.

diagram 1

4 Carefully separate the top fabric pieces from the bottom fabric pieces, keeping them in the same order. Rearrange the strips so that pieces 1, 3 and 5 of the top fabric are teamed up with 2 and 4 of the bottom fabric and 1,3 and 5 of the bottom fabric are teamed with 2 and 4 of the top fabric. These will be the first two blocks (diagram 2).

diagram 2

5 Stitch the four seams in each block and press the seams carefully to one side. Repeat with the remaining pairs to make a total of thirty-six blocks.

6 To complete the blocks, trim them all square. The precise size is not important but they must all be the same! The blocks in my quilt were trimmed to 8½ in/21 cm square but fabric widths do vary a little and you may find that yours are big enough to trim to 9 in/22 cm square.

7 Arrange thirty-five of the blocks in seven rows of five following the quilt assembly plan on page 66 (save the last block to make a label for the back of the quilt). If you are shading the colours across the quilt, play with various layouts until you are happy with the arrangement.

8 Stitch the blocks in each row together, pressing the seams in opposite directions on alternate rows as you go, then stitch the rows together – the seams that were pressed in alternate directions should now butt together to ensure a good match. Press well.

ADDING THE BORDERS
If you have shaded your quilt top, follow steps 1 to 5, if you have randomly pieced the blocks, follow steps 6 to 9.

1 Pin the quilt top on a design board or lay it out flat. Using the 5 in/12.5 cm strips of fabric that you

set aside, arrange the various colours roughly around the edges – you may find it easier to cut the strips in half. Decide where to make the joins, so that the colours shade around the quilt in line, more or less, with the colours in the quilt top – this is not an exact science!

2 Measure the width of the quilt through the centre and join enough pieces together to make the top and bottom border sections. The joins can be made at right angles in the usual way or at a 45 degree angle. The angles look good if they slant in the same direction as the shading. To make an angled join, position two strips at right angles to each other, with right sides together. Draw a line across the corner at 45 degrees and stitch on the line. Trim the excess fabric off the corner and press the seam open (diagram 3).

diagram 3

3 After joining the border sections, check the width and trim if necessary. Stitch the top and bottom border sections to the quilt top. Press the seams towards the borders.

4 Measure the length of the quilt including the borders and join enough 5 in/12.5 cm strips as before to make the side border sections.

5 After joining check the length and trim if necessary. Stitch the side border sections to the quilt. Press the seams towards the borders, then press the whole quilt top and proceed to applying the spirals.

6 Measure the width of the quilt through the centre. Cut the 5 in/12.5 cm border strips to various lengths (anything between about 6 and 18 in/15 and 50 cm). Join enough pieces together (using the colours randomly) to make the top and bottom border sections. Press the seams open.

7 After joining, check the width and trim if necessary. Stitch the top and bottom border sections to the quilt top. Press the seams towards the borders.

8 Measure the length of the quilt including the borders and join enough pieces together as before to make the side border sections.

9 After joining check the length and trim if necessary. Stitch the side border sections to the quilt. Press the seams towards the borders, then press the whole quilt top.

APPLYING THE SPIRALS

1 Trace twelve large spirals and twelve small spirals from the templates opposite onto the paper side of the fusible webbing.

2 Cut out around the outside of the spirals leaving a small margin around each one.

3 Iron the spirals onto the back of the green and orange fabrics: six large and six small in each colour. Cut out along the lines.

4 Arrange the spirals on the quilt and when you are happy with the layout, peel the paper backing off and iron them in place.

5 To avoid puckering, place a piece of "Stitch and Tear" behind each spiral, then stitch around the edges of the spirals to secure them. We used a zig-zag stitch and matching threads. Alternatively you could use a straight stitch, a satin stitch or a blanket stitch. You could also try decorative threads. Make an extra spiral and iron it on to some spare fabric so that you can experiment first.

6 After all the spirals have been stitched, remove the "Stitch and Tear" carefully from the back.

FINISHING

1 Spread the backing right side down on a flat surface, then smooth the wadding and the pieced top, right side up, on top. Fasten together with safety pins or baste in a grid.

2 Machine or hand quilt in the pattern of your choice.

NOTE "Glow Worms" has been machine quilted on "Bertha", the long arm quilting machine at "The Bramble Patch" with a large "vermicelli" pattern all over the background blocks. The spirals were simply outlined. Alternatively, you could quilt by hand or machine to emphasize the angled lines of the blocks.

3 Take the nine 2 in/5 cm strips of blue fabric and cut them into a variety of shorter lengths (anything from 6 to 18 in/15 to 50 cm long). Rejoin the sections of binding at 45 degrees as for the border strips – you can either shade the colours to flow around the quilt or join randomly (as with the border strips). Trim the excess fabric off the corners, then press the seams open.

4 Fold the binding in half along the length and use to bind the quilt with a double-fold binding mitred at the corners.

5 Don't forget to add a label to your quilt!

templates - full size

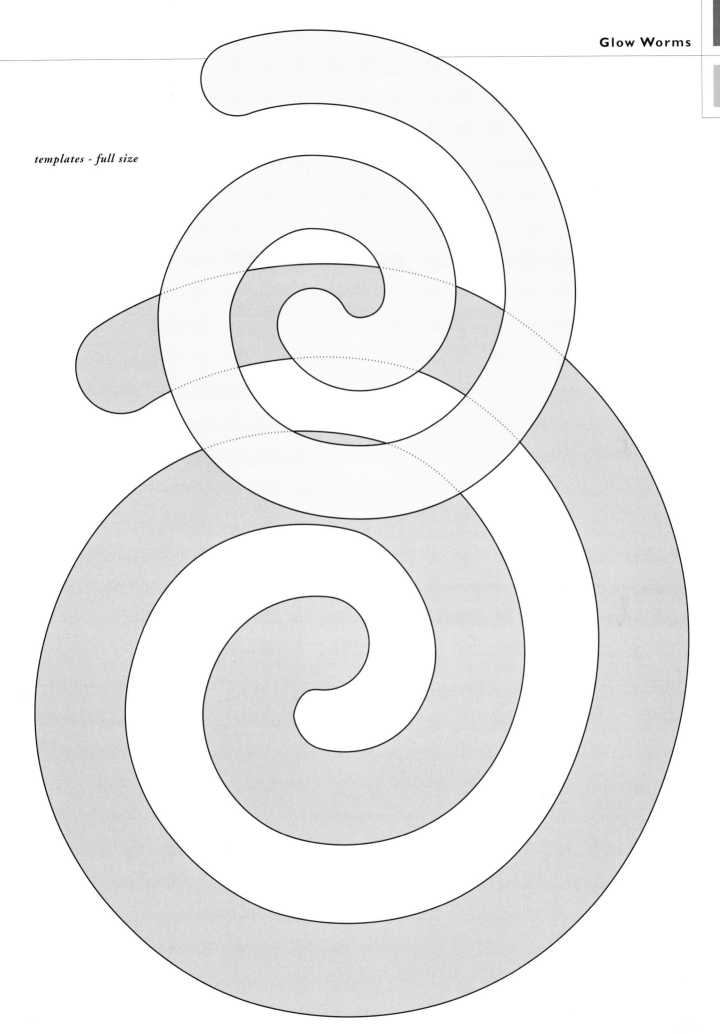

Aurora

Designed by Jean Hunt

The inspiration for this lap quilt came from the wonderful fabric, which is produced in a spectrum of glowing colours. The block design developed from our attempts to use as many of the colours as possible in one quilt. After the quilting was completed, when we stood back and looked at it, we could see lots of little sailing boats on a higgledy-piggledy sea! This was an unexpected bonus, however this would depend on what fabric you used. Because it is made up of blocks, the quilt could easily be made larger by adding more blocks – but you will obviously need to buy more fabric. We used a twin needle sewing machine for the quilting but this is optional.

Finished size: 36 x 48 in/93 x 122 cm

MATERIALS
All fabrics used in the quilt top are 45 in/115 cm
wide, 100% cotton

Fabrics: 6 x ½ yd/50 cm of toning or graded fabrics, or
1 yd/1 m of "feature" fabric and 4 x ½ yd/50 cm of
complementary fabric.

Binding: 6 in/15 cm of fabric cut across the bolt
Stiff card
Tracing or freezer paper
Quilter's pencil
Wadding: 2 oz polyester, 40 x 52 in/103 x 132 cm
Backing: cotton fabric, 40 x 52 in/103 x 132 cm
Variegated machine quilting thread

ALTERNATIVE COLOUR SCHEMES

The triangle at the centre of the block provides a "window" into which you could put a feature fabric if desired but take care when using directional fabrics as the blocks are twisted around in different directions before being stitched together. A random all-over print would be fine. You could use either a contrast or a blend as the examples here show.

1

2

3

4

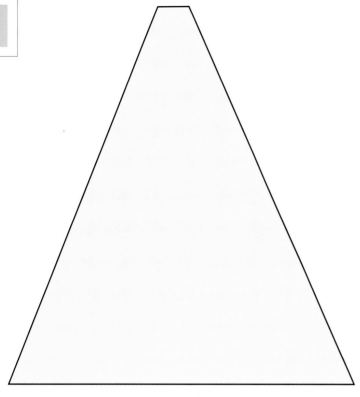

template

CUTTING

1 Trace off the triangle template above and stick to a piece of stiff card. Cut out from the card as accurately as possible. Note that the ¼ in/0.75 cm seam allowance is already included in the template.

2 Cut a 4 in/10 cm strip from your chosen central or feature fabric. Following the cutting plan (diagram 1), draw round the triangle template using a quilter's pencil, you will need 48 triangles altogether. Cut out the triangles.

diagram 1

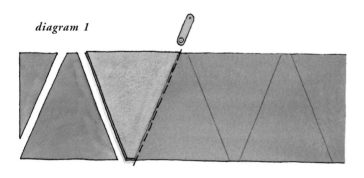

3 Cut the outer strips from the remaining fabrics, using a rotary cutter. For each block you will need: two 3½ x 6 in/9 x 15 cm strips, one 3½"x 9 in/9 x 23 cm strip. As there are 48 blocks you will need to cut the above sets 48 times in total. To save time, cut a long 3½ in/9 cm strip from your chosen fabric, then cut this to the desired length, when required.

4 For the binding; cut the 6 in/15 cm strip into four 1½ in/3.75 cm strips.

STITCHING

1 Take one of the triangles and one 3½ x 6 in/9 x 15 cm strip. Place the strip right side up and lay the triangle on top, right side down, no more than ½ in/1.5 cm from the top of the strip (diagram 2). Pin and stitch the seam and press towards the strip.

diagram 2

2 Lay the second 3½ x 6 in/9 x 15 cm strip on top of the other long edge of the triangle, right sides together, taking in the top of the first strip stitched. Pin and stitch the seam, then press as before. Using the rotary cutter, trim off the excess fabric level with the bottom of the triangle (diagram 3).

diagram 3

3 Take the 3½ x 9 in/9 x 23 cm strip and place over the straight edge just cut, right sides together. Pin and stitch, then press the completed block unit.

4 Using a 6½ in square rotary ruler, cut a square from the block unit, making sure that the central triangle is not cut (diagram 4). Repeat this to make a total of 48 squares. You will notice that by turning the square at random before cutting (making sure you stay within the boundaries of the block unit), you will achieve a slightly different looking block each time, this is what forms the character of the quilt.

diagram 4

NOTE If you don't have a square ruler, draw a 6½ in/16.5 cm square from card, cut a "window" in the centre to help with the positioning, and use this together with a soluble marker to mark your cutting line.

5 When you have completed and pressed your 48 blocks, lay them out on the floor in eight rows of six following the quilt assembly plan on page 74. Move around the blocks until you are happy with the layout.

6 Stitch the blocks together in horizontal rows, following the layout, taking a ¼ in/0.75 cm seam allowance. When you have completed the rows, press, and stitch the rows together, starting at the top. This completes the pieced top. Press lightly.

FINISHING

1 Measure the pieced top, and cut the wadding and backing fabric at least ½ in/1.5 cm bigger on all sides.

2 Spread the backing right side down on a flat surface, then smooth the wadding and the patchwork top, right side up on top. Fasten together with safety pins or baste in a grid.

3 If you have a twin needle sewing machine, thread with variegated thread and following the photograph above, stitch two short lines of quilting on each block. Alternatively, stitch two parallel lines. Cut the thread long enough to stitch in afterwards (or, for speed, use the lockstitch found on some sewing machines). Then quilt "in-the-ditch" using the same variegated thread, but this is optional.

4 When the quilting is complete, stitch the binding strips together in one long strip and use to bind the edges of the quilt with a double-fold binding, mitred at the corners. Finally, add a label.

Sevens and Nines

Designed by Rosemary Wilkinson

This bright quilt is designed to be made from fat quarters in prints with a large piece of plain fabric to set off the colours. It's based on the nine-patch block but uses only seven pieces. These are arranged randomly with plain filling squares at irregular intervals. This size of quilt makes a cheerful topper for a child's bed or a throw for a sunny conservatory. It can easily be made larger, either by adding more blocks or by increasing the size of each block.

Finished size: 45 x 57 in/113 x 143 cm

MATERIALS
All fabrics in the quilt top are 45 in/115 cm wide, 100% cotton

Small squares: 6 fat quarters in red, orange and pink small print patterns

Strips, large squares, border and binding: yellow, 1¾ yds/1.60 m

Backing: pink small print, 1¾ yds/1.60 m

Wadding: 2 oz polyester, 1¾ yds/1.60 m

Coton perlé: red and orange

Large-eyed needle

ALTERNATIVE COLOUR SCHEMES

1 For a vibrant quilt use hand-dyed fabrics in the colours of the rainbow. 2 Soft and small floral prints set against calico make a very pretty, cottagey colour scheme. 3 A mix of regular and irregular dotted patterns in muted colours produce a harmonious design suitable for either traditional or contemporary homes. 4 Blue and white always make a crisp and clean combination.

1

2

3

4

CUTTING

1 From each fat quarter, cut seven strips across the width, 2½ in/6.5 cm deep.

2 From the yellow fabric, cut ten strips across the width, 2½ in/6.5 cm deep; cut two strips across the width, 6½ in/16.5 cm deep; then cross-cut into 8 squares; cut five strips 2½ in/6.5 cm wide for the binding; reserve the remainder for the borders.

STITCHING

1 Place two of the fat quarter strips right sides together and stitch down one long side, taking a ¼ in/0.75 cm seam allowance.

2 Place a third strip right side down along one long edge of the unit just made and stitch as before.

3 Repeat with the remaining three fat quarter strips. Press the seams one way on the first set and the opposite way on the second.

4 Cross-cut both units into 2½ in/6.5 cm strips (diagram 1).

diagram 1

5 Chain-piece the two different short strips together in pairs. Cut, open out and press.

6 Place one of the 2½ in/6.5 cm yellow strips on top of one of the units made in step 5, aligning raw edges and stitch. Without cutting the yellow strip, add another unit underneath and stitch. Continue chain-piecing in this way until all the six-square units have been stitched to yellow strips (diagram 2).

diagram 2

7 Trim the yellow strips level with each six-square unit, open out and press (diagram 3).

diagram 3

8 Following the quilt assembly plan on page 80, lay out the blocks interspersed with single yellow squares in your preferred arrangement, with seven blocks across and nine down.

9 Working on the two vertical rows on the lefthand side of the arrangement, chain-piece the blocks together in pairs (diagram 4). Cut, open out and press the pairs of squares, then replace in the correct positions in the quilt plan.

diagram 4

10 Repeat with vertical rows three and four, then with five and six.

11 Stitch the units together in horizontal rows, then pin and stitch the horizontal rows together, being careful to match the seams.

ADDING THE BORDERS

1 Measure the pieced top through the centre from side to side, then cut two strips to this measurement and 1½ in/4 cm deep from the remaining yellow fabric. Stitch to the top and bottom of the quilt.

2 Measure the pieced top through the centre from top to bottom, then cut two strips to this measurement, 1½ in/4 cm deep, from the remaining yellow fabric, joined as necessary. Stitch to the sides.

FINISHING

1 Give your backing and the pieced top a good press, then spread the backing right side down on a flat surface. Smooth the wadding and the pieced top, right side up, on top. Fasten together with safety pins or baste in a grid.

2 Using coton perlé threaded into a large eye needle, tie the quilt at the intersection of each block, alternating the red and orange threads.

3 Join the binding strips into a continuous length long enough to go all round the edge of the quilt and use to bind the quilt with a double-fold binding, mitred at the corners.

Stripes and Spots

Designed by Dorothy Wood

The use of bold stripes and spot fabric has transformed this simple design into a stunningly colourful quilt. Instead of quilting by hand or machine, the quilt is tied together at regular intervals. As the rectangular patchwork pieces are speed cut using a rotary cutter, the quilt top can be pieced together in a few hours. Because the design is so simple, you can easily alter the shape and size of the quilt by adding or subtracting rows or columns of blocks.

Finished size: 51½ x 80 in/131 x 204 cm

MATERIALS

All fabrics used in the quilt top are 45 in/115 cm wide 100% cotton. Backing fabric is 59 in/150 cm wide.

Yellow and white striped cotton fabric: 1¾ yds/1.50 m

Blue and white striped cotton fabric: 1¾ yds/1.50 m
Yellow and blue spot cotton fabric: 2¾ yds/2.50 m
Backing: white, 59 x 86½ in/150 x 220 cm
Wadding: 2 oz polyester, 59 x 86½ in/150 x 220 cm
White sewing thread
Large-eyed needle
Coton perlé: dark blue no. 5

ALTERNATIVE COLOUR SCHEMES

1 The classic blue and white is always popular. Choose fabrics of similar weight but with different textures. 2 Because the fish motif fabric is so busy, only one plain batik fabric has been used. This creates larger areas of one fabric and pulls the design together. 3 Checks and plaids give an instant country feel. Choose a plain fabric that tones with the background colour of the checks. 4 Ideal for a ballet loving teenager, two pretty pastels have been picked out from the ballet shoe fabric to create a harmonious, muted quilt.

1

2

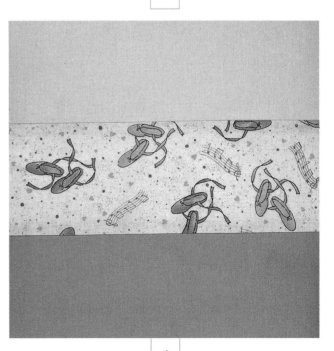

3

4

CUTTING

1 Cut a 2¾ yd/2.5 m strip, 12 in/30 cm wide from one long edge of the yellow and blue spot fabric and set to one side. This piece will be used later to bind the quilt.

2 Press the remaining blue spot fabric and fold in half crosswise, then in half again. Steam-press the fabric bundle and lift onto the cutting mat. Using a rotary cutter and ruler, cut five strips across the width, 4 in/10 cm wide, then cross-cut into forty 10¾ in/27 cm rectangles.

3 Fold the striped fabrics in half crosswise once only and check that the stripes are straight on each layer. Cut ten strips across the width, 4 in/10 cm wide, then cross-cut into forty 10¾ in/27 cm rectangles.

NOTE Take extra care when folding and pressing the striped fabric to make sure that the stripes are straight on each layer before cutting.

STITCHING

1 Place a yellow striped strip on top of a yellow and blue spot strip with right sides facing. Stitch the seam with a ¼ in/0.75cm seam allowance. Stitch a blue stripe strip to the other edge of the spotted strip (diagram 1). Press the seam allowances towards the striped fabric on each side. Make all forty blocks in the same way. You could chain-piece these to speed up the process.

diagram 1

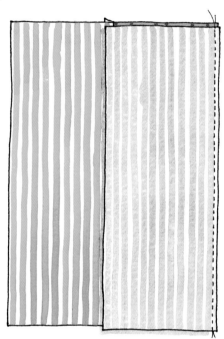

2 Check that each of the blocks is absolutely square by measuring on the cutting mat and trim slightly if necessary. Lay five blocks in a row, alternating the stripes from horizontal to vertical. Keep the blue stripes to the lefthand side on the vertical blocks and to the bottom of the horizontal blocks throughout. Lay out all the blocks as shown in the quilt assembly plan on page 86.

3 Stitch each row of blocks together with ¼ in/0.75 cm seams. Press the seams towards the striped fabric.

4 Pin the rows together matching the seams carefully. If the seams were pressed in the right direction, the seam allowances should lie in opposite directions where they meet. Stitch the seams taking the usual seam allowance and press all the seams towards one end of the pieced top.

FINISHING

1 Spread the backing right side down on a flat surface, then smooth the wadding and the pieced top, right side up, on top.

2 Baste around the pieced top through all the layers, ½ in/1.5 cm from the edge. Pin through all layers at each corner of the blocks.

3 To tie the quilt, thread a length of dark blue coton perlé onto the large eye needle. Take a small stitch through all layers where the seams meet at the corner of the first block, pull the thread through leaving a 1 in/2.5 cm tail. Take a back stitch and then trim the other tail the same length (diagram 2). Pull the ends tight and tie in a reef (flat) knot. Trim the ends to ¼ in/0.75 cm.

diagram 2

4 Stitch and tie with coton perlé at each pin. Lay the quilt out flat again. Use the quilter's ruler to find the centre of each spot fabric strip and mark with a pin through all layers. Stitch and tie with perlé cotton at each pin.

5 Lay the quilt flat and smooth out carefully. Tuck a cutting mat under one edge of the quilt. Using the quilter's ruler and rotary cutter, trim the excess wadding and backing fabric ¾ in/2 cm from the edge of the quilt top. Move the cutting mat as required and cut the same measurement all the way round.

6 Cut four 2¾ yd/2.5 m, 2½ in/6.5 cm wide strips from the reserved yellow and blue spot fabric. Press the strips, then fold under and press a ¼ in/0.75 cm turning along one long side of each strip.

7 Pin the unpressed edge of one strip along the top edge of the quilt top, right sides together and aligning the raw edges. Machine stitch ¼ in/0.75 cm from the edge of the fabric though all layers. Trim level with the wadding and backing at the ends. Pin and stitch a second strip along the bottom edge of the quilt in the same way.

8 Fold the binding over to the reverse side. Slipstitch the pressed turning to the machine stitching.

9 Pin the remaining strips down the side edges, leaving ½ in/1.5 cm of fabric jutting out at either end and machine stitch (diagram 3). Turn in the excess fabric at each end, then fold the binding to the reverse. Slipstitch all the edges to complete the quilt.

diagram 3

Moulin Rouge

Designed by Claire Higgott

Moulin Rouge is made with the Mary's Triangle block – a deceptively simple block which can be twisted and turned to produce dozens of different quilt designs. The relatively large pieces of the block make it perfect for showing off bold fabrics as in this stunning single bed quilt but it also works well with more subtle colours. The blocks are quick and simple to construct using only squares and rectangles.

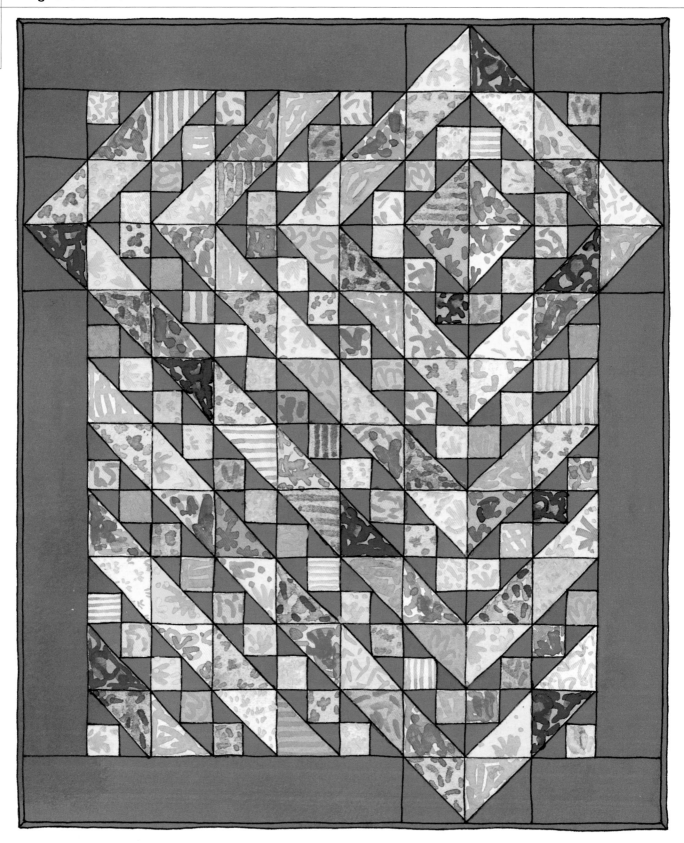

Finished size: 60 x 72 in/153 cm x 183 cm

FABRIC REQUIREMENTS
All fabrics used in the quilt top are 45 in/115 cm wide.

Blocks, border and binding: red, 2¾ yds/2.50 m
Pink and green prints: 12 fat quarters, 6 different patterns in a mixture of these two colours
Backing: red print, 66 x 78 in/168 x 198 cm
Wadding: lightweight, 66 x 78 in/168 x 198 cm

ALTERNATIVE COLOUR SCHEMES

1 Softly coloured batik and marble fabrics give a gentler look to the design.
2 The pretty floral and fairy prints look crisp and summery teamed with white.
3 The large triangles are big enough to showcase bright novelty prints. Instead
of using just one fabric for the rectangles, this colourway uses a variety of bright
fabrics which become the small "background" triangles when the block is completed. 4 The skin prints and abstract stripe have a slightly African feel to them
and the colours really glow against the black background.

1

2

3

4

CUTTING

(Cut strips selvage to selvage unless otherwise indicated.)

1 From the red fabric,

cut nine 3½ in/9 cm strips, then sub-cut into a total of eighty 3½ x 4½ in/9 x 11.5 cm rectangles;

cut six 6½ in/16.5 cm strips; from one of these strips, cut four 6½ x 7½ in/16.5 x 19 cm rectangles for the border blocks;

from the next strip, cut two 6½ x 12½ in/16.5 x 31.5 cm rectangles and two 6½ in/16.5 cm squares for the border;

cut two pieces, 6½ x 36½ in/16.5 x 91.5 cm from the third and fourth strips for the border;

cut two pieces, 6½ x 42½ in/16.5 x 106.5 cm from the fifth and sixth strips for the border.

The remaining red fabric will be used for the binding.

2 From each of the twelve fat quarter prints cut seven 3½ in/9 cm squares and four 6½ x 7½ in/16.5 x 19 cm rectangles. This allows a few extra pieces. Set aside the spare 6½ x 7½ in/16.5 x 19 cm rectangles as some of them will be needed for the border blocks.

STITCHING

(Use a ¼ in/0.75 cm seam allowance throughout.)

1 Stitch each of the 3½ in/9 cm printed squares to a 3½ x 4½ in/9 x 11.5 cm red rectangle. Press the seam towards the rectangle.

2 Take two of the new units, turn one upside down and stitch to the first (diagram 1). It doesn't matter what colour the squares are as they will end up in different blocks.

diagram 1

3 Snip the seam allowance in the centre and press each half of the seam towards the red rectangles.

4 On the wrong side draw stitching lines as shown by the pencil lines (diagram 2). The lines should pass through the inner corners of the squares.

diagram 2

6½ in/16.5cm

6½ in/16.5cm

5 Repeat with remaining pieced units to make a total of forty of these pieced units. Pair one of these units with a 6½ x 7½ in/16.5 x 19 cm print rectangle, right sides together – this print should be different from the small squares. Pin and stitch along both of the marked stitching lines.

Cut between the stitched lines. The seam allowances can be trimmed to ¼ in/0.75 cm. Open each half out and press the seams towards the large print triangles to make two Mary's Triangle blocks (diagram 3).

diagram 3

6 Repeat to make a total of eighty blocks.

7 Arrange the blocks in ten rows of eight following the quilt assembly plan on page 92.

8 Stitch the blocks in each row together, pressing the seams in opposite directions on alternate rows as you go. Then stitch the rows together – the seams should now butt together. Press. The quilt top should measure 48½ x 60½ in/121.5 x 151.5 cm at this stage.

ADDING THE BORDERS

1 To make the border blocks, choose four of the spare 6½ x 7½ in/16.5 x 19 cm print rectangles and pair each with a red one, right sides together. Draw stitching lines as shown in diagram 4.

diagram 4

6½ in/16.5cm

6½ in/16.5cm

2 Stitch along the lines. Cut between the lines, open up and press to make eight border blocks.

3 Sort the eight border blocks into four pairs, varying the prints in each pair. Stitch the pairs of border blocks together so that the print fabrics form peaks.

4 Following the quilt assembly plan, assemble the four border sections. Stitch each border and press the

seams. As you complete each border, pin a label (left, right, top and bottom) to it as they are all different!

5 Stitch the side borders onto the pieced top, making sure that the border blocks line up accurately with the blocks in the top. Press the seams towards the borders. Stitch the top and bottom borders to the quilt and press as before.

FINISHING

1 Spread the backing right side down on a flat surface, then smooth the wadding and the pieced top, right side up, on top. Fasten together with safety pins or baste in a grid.

2 Machine or hand quilt in the pattern of your choice.

NOTE

Moulin Rouge has been machine quilted on "Bertha", the long arm quilting machine at "The Bramble Patch" using an edge-to-edge design. It would also look good quilted by hand or machine "in-the-ditch" to emphasize the diagonal lines.

3 From the remaining red fabric, cut seven 2 in/5 cm strips, selvage to selvage. Trim off the selvages, then join the strips of binding with 45 degree seams. Trim off the excess fabric, then press the seams open. The angled seam helps to spread the bulk of the join.

4 Fold the binding in half along the length and use to bind the quilt with a double-fold binding mitred at the corners. Don't forget to add a label to your quilt!

All Fenced In

Designed by Sarah Wellfair

After spending a few days helping my son Nick to make his first quilt using the rail fence pattern, I decided to try to take the traditional block and make it more interesting. First I put it on point, then fenced it in with triangles and finally sashed it together. The resulting lap quilt was very quick and easy to make using quick piecing and rotary equipment.

Finished size: 58 x 58 in/147 x 147 cm

MATERIALS

All fabrics used in the quilt top are 45 in/115 cm
wide, 100% cotton
Square blocks: orange, 20 in/55 cm; yellow,
20 in/55 cm

Triangles and sashing squares: blue, 40 in/1.10 m
Sashing strips: gold, 42 in/1.10 m
Binding: orange, 20 in/50 cm
Backing: blue, 3¼ yds/3 m
Wadding: 2 oz polyester, 60 x 60 in/152 x 152 cm
Threads: to match fabrics for quilting

ALTERNATIVE COLOUR SCHEMES

1 The small floral prints merge together to give the impression of one flowery fabric. 2 The chicken novelty print makes this into a fun quilt for a child. 3 Pretty pinks and creams would suit a country cottage bedroom. 4 A harmonious matching of mauve and purple checks and floral prints produces an elegant colourway.

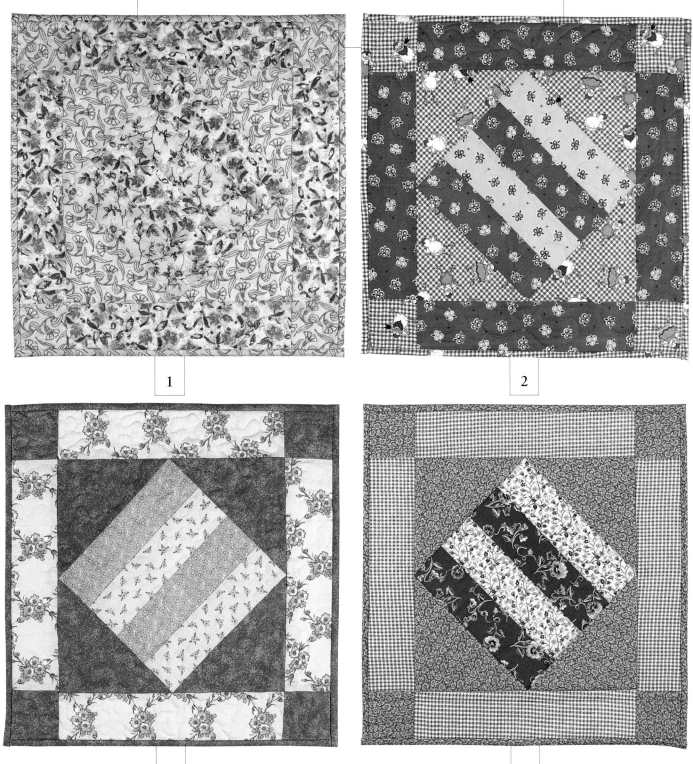

1

2

3

4

CUTTING

1 From the orange fabric, cut 8 strips 2½ in/6.5 cm deep across the full width of fabric.

2 From the yellow fabric, cut 8 strips 2½ in/6.5 cm deep across the full width of fabric.

3 From the blue fabric for the triangles and sashing squares, cut 16 squares 9¼ x 9¼ in/ 23.5 x 23.5 cm and cross-cut each one into four quarter-square triangles; cut 25 squares, 3 x 3 in/7.5 x 7.5 cm.

STITCHING

1 Take one orange and one yellow strip and place right sides together, then stitch together down one long side, taking a ¼ in/0.75 cm seam allowance. Do the same to the remaining seven orange and seven yellow strips.

2 Take two of the pairs and place right sides together with an orange strip on top of a yellow one. Stitch together down one long side, taking the usual seam allowance, so that you have four strips of alternate colours. Repeat with the remaining strips. You should now have four pieces with four strips in each. Press the seams towards the darker fabric. These strips should now measure approximately 8½ in/21.5 cm deep.

3 Using rotary cutter and ruler, cross-cut the strips into 8½ in/21.5 cm squares. This should make 20 squares – you will need 16 of these for your quilt.

4 Stitch one of the quarter square blue triangles to the top and bottom of each orange and yellow square (diagram 1). Do the same on the other two sides. Press the seams towards the blue triangles.

diagram 1

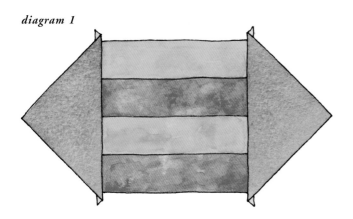

5 Arrange these squares in four rows, four across following the quilt assembly plan on page 98.

6 Measure across middle of each square and take an average measurement. Cut 40 sashing strips from the gold fabric to this length and 3 in/7.5 cm wide.

7 Stitch one sashing strip to the top of each square, then stitch the squares together in vertical rows.

8 Stitch one sashing strip to the end of each row (diagram 2). You should now have four rows of four blocks with sashing in between.

diagram 2   *diagram 3*

9 Take the rest of the sashing strips and stitch one small blue square to the end of each strip, then stitch the strips together into five lengths. Finally take the five remaining small blue squares and stitch one to the end of each length (diagram 3). Press all the seams towards the gold sashing.

10 Stitch the sashing strips to the left side of each of the four rows of blocks, then stitch the rows together. Stitch the last sashing strip to the righthand edge of the pieced top. Press the top for the last time and cut off any unwanted threads.

FINISHING

1 Measure the pieced top through the centre from side to side and cut and join the backing fabric to this size plus 2 in/5 cm on all sides.

2 Spread the backing right side down on a flat surface, then smooth the wadding and the pieced top, right side up, on top. Fasten together with safety pins or baste in a grid.

3 Quilt as desired. I used a three step zig-zag in the sashings and free quilted in the blocks.

4 Trim the excess backing and wadding level with the pieced top.

5 Cut the binding fabric across the width into strips, 3 in/7.5 cm deep and stitch across the short sides, right sides together, to form one long length of binding. Fold in half, wrong sides together along the length and press.

6 Measure the quilt through the centre from side to side and cut two strips of binding to this length. Pin one of these to the top of the quilt, matching raw edges and stitch taking a ¼ in/0.75 cm seam allowance. Repeat at the bottom of the quilt.

7 Turn each binding strip to the back of the quilt and slip stitch to the quilt covering the stitching line.

8 Measure the quilt through the centre from top to bottom and cut bindings to this length plus 1½ in/4 cm. Pin one of these binding strips to the left-hand side of the quilt, overlapping by ¾ in/2 cm at each end. Stitch taking the usual seam allowance.

9 Fold in the short ends, turn the binding strip to the back and slipstitch down as before (diagram 4). Repeat to bind the righthand side of the quilt.

diagram 4

10 Your quilt is now ready to be signed and dated.

Treasures Cot Quilt

Designed by Gail Smith

The treasures cot quilt was so called because of the bright fabrics used and also the treasured baby that it might be made for. Babies grow, however, and this simple block-by-block quilt, grows very quickly too, so that it could be easily made larger than the example shown here which is made up of twelve blocks. It could also be made from scraps or a fat quarter collection.

Finished size: 33 x 43 in/79.5 x 103.5 cm

MATERIALS

All fabrics used in the quilt top are 45 in/115 cm wide, 100% cotton.

Four-patch centre squares and outer border: a long quarter (¼ yd or 25 cm) across the bolt of at least seven different bright fabrics.

Border round each four patch-centre: assuming you will use each fabric for two blocks, 6 in/15 cm strips cut across the bolt of six toning or contrasting fabrics

Binding: 6 in/15 cm of chosen fabric, cut across the bolt

Backing: butterfly print cotton or sheeting, 36 x 45 in/91 x 115 cm

Wadding: 2 oz polyester or a cotton alternative, 36 x 45 in/91 x 115 cm

Variegated machine thread: either rayon or cotton

ALTERNATIVE COLOUR SCHEMES

The Treasures Cot Quilt design will lend itself to lots of different fabrics: brights, plains or traditional patterns will sit comfortably together as shown in the four different colourways below. Why not try soft fleece on the back as an alternative to the wadding and cotton backing?

1

2

3

4

CUTTING

1 From each of the fabrics chosen for the centre squares of the blocks and the outer border, cut one 3 in/7.5 cm strip. Cross-cut the strips into 3 in/7.5 cm squares. Put these to one side.

2 From each of the six fabrics that border the four-patch centres, cut one 3 in/7.5 cm strip across the width.

3 Cut the binding fabric into 1½ in/4 cm strips.

4 Do not cut the backing until you have finished stitching.

STITCHING

1 Jumble the squares in a carrier bag and select, at random, two squares at a time to stitch together with ¼ in/0.75 cm seam allowance. Using the chain-piecing method, stitch 24 pairs of squares together. (I usually peek to make sure that no two are the same!) Reserve the rest of the squares until later. When you have your 24 pairs, cut to separate, open out and press the seams to one side.

2 Next, again choosing at random, stitch two sets of pairs together, 12 times, giving 12 mini four-patch blocks (diagram 1). Press all the seams to one side. (Keep the remaining squares for the outer border.)

diagram 1

3 To add borders to each four-patch block, take a 3 x 45 in/7.5 x 115 cm strip of your chosen fabric and place it on top of a four-patch block aligning raw edges and right sides together. Stitch, then trim level with the edge of the four-patch block (diagram 2).

diagram 2

4 Repeat to add another strip to the bottom of the block (diagram 3). Press the seams towards the darker fabric.

diagram 3

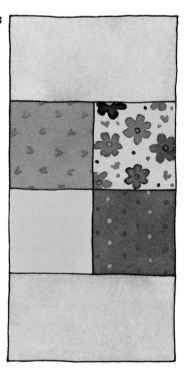

NOTE
To speed up this process, you could stitch all the top border pieces first, then all the bottom pieces.

5 Repeat to add the border strip to the sides of the blocks (diagram 4). Press.

diagram 4

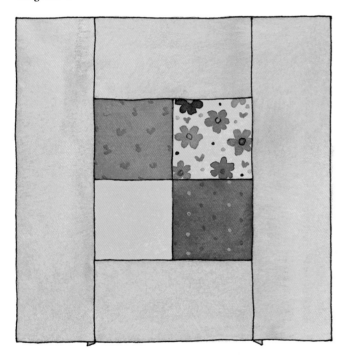

6 Lay the completed blocks on the floor, all the same way up (short border to the top), following the quilt assembly plan on page 104. Try different layouts until you are happy with this and try not to have two blocks the same or similar next to each other.

7 Stitch three blocks together in a strip. Repeat to make four strips. Press.

8 Working down from the top, stitch the first strip to the second, then add the third and fourth, as in your layout. When complete, press lightly.

ADDING THE BORDERS

1 Taking the 3 in/7.5 cm squares left over from the first stage, at random, stitch enough of these together to make two strips long enough for the sides and two for the top and bottom borders – this should be 18 squares for the sides and 12 for the top and bottom of the pieced top. Chain-piece in pairs if you wish to speed up the process. Press.

2 Stitch a border strip to the top and bottom of the quilt, then to each side. You have now completed your quilt top.

FINISHING

1 Measure the completed quilt top, and cut wadding and backing fabric at least ½ in/1.5 cm bigger on all sides.

2 Spread the backing right side down on a flat surface, then smooth the wadding and the pieced top, right side up, on top. Fasten together with safety pins or baste in a grid.

3 Using a walking foot and the decorative stitches on your sewing machine, ideally a scallop or wave pattern, quilt in lines down and across the quilt, as desired.

4 Join the binding strips into one length long enough to go all round the quilt and use to bind the quilt with a single-fold binding, mitred at the corners.

Country Coverlet

Designed by Gill Turley

A cheerful quilt made from oddments of checked and striped cottons and edged with a crisp border of prairie points. The felt coin dots plus the borders of bright triangles pick out the colours from the checks used in the centre section. This simple quilt looks fantastic as a top quilt over a plain cream counterpane or sheet. Alternatively, it would make a great throw over the back of a sofa. It's hand quilted with coton à broder thread but for speed the quilting could be done by machine. Ties secure the quilt layers in the centre section and these are stitched through the decorative coin dots.

Finished size: 56 x 40 in/145 x 100 cm (including the prairie points edging)

MATERIALS

Large check fabric for centre rectangles: four pieces, each measuring 18½ x 14½ in/46.5 x 36.5 cm (pieces **1**, **2**, **3** and **4**)

Striped fabric for centre strips, top and bottom borders: two 18½ x 4½ in/46.5 x 11.5 cm (pieces **a** and **b**); two co-ordinating pieces 14½ x 4½ in/36.5 x 11.5 cm (pieces **c** and **d**);

For centre square: one piece 4½ x 4½ in/11.5 x 11.5 cm (piece **e**)

Border triangles: bright striped and checked cottons in assorted colours:
thirteen light/medium squares, 5 x 5 in/13 x 13 cm

thirteen dark squares, 5 x 5 in/13 x 13 cm

Border strips: darker checked fabric:
two long strips, 16½ x 4½ in/41.5 x 11.5 cm
two short strips, 12½ x 4½ in/31.5 x 11.5 cm

Striped fabric for top and bottom outer borders: two pieces each 40½ x 4½ in/101.5 x 11.5 cm

Prairie points edging: lightweight fabric, one strip, 40 x 8 in/100 x 20 cm

Felt for coin dots: washable felt in assorted colours: four pieces 12 x 12 in/30 x 30 cm

Backing: small check, 60 x 44 in/150 x 110 cm

Wadding: cotton, 60 x 44 in/155 x 110 cm

Thread for quilting and ties: coton à broder no. 16 or similar

Large quilting hoop (optional)

Large-eyed needle

ALTERNATIVE COLOUR SCHEMES

1 Earth colours of brown, ochre, rust and gold blend together well and create a warm look. Bright red coin dots set off the flowery print. 2 Soft checks, stripes and dots enhance the ladybird fabric chosen for the centre section. Triangles in red and green plus a strip of flame red add warmth. 3 Framed by strips of jewel coloured fabric the pink and cream flower trellis makes an interesting choice for the centre. The rich pink triangles placed next to the soft cream ones add strength. 4 Fresh blue, green and white fabrics provide a crisp look. These are mainly stripes and checks but small prints work well in the triangles.

1

2

3

4

STITCHING

1 To make the central section, stitch pieces **1** and **2** to centre strip **a** and pieces **3** and **4** to strip **b**. Press the seams towards the strips. Stitch centre strips **c** and **d** to centre square **e**, pressing the seams away from the square. Next join the top section to the bottom section with the centre strip in the middle. Press these seams away from the centre strip (diagram 1).

diagram 1

2 To make the triangle units for the borders, place the thirteen dark and thirteen light/medium squares right sides together, pairing light/medium squares with dark squares. Draw a pencil line diagonally from corner to corner, then stitch on each side of the diagonal line ¼ in/0.75 cm away from pencil marking (diagram 2). For speed these units can be chain-pieced.

diagram 2

3 When the stitching stage has been completed, snip the squares apart, then cut along the pencil lines. Press these units open making sure that the seams are pressed towards the darker fabric. Trim the pieced units to the correct size, 4½ x 4½ in/11.5 x 11.5 cm.

ADDING THE BORDERS

1 For the top and bottom borders, join together six triangle units and press the seams towards the dark fabric. Add the short border strips of darker checked fabric to complete. Press the seams towards the strips (diagram 3).

diagram 3

2 For each of the side borders, join together seven triangle units and press seams as before. To each side border now add a long border strip of darker checked fabric.

3 Pin one of the side borders to the lefthand edge of the quilt with the triangle section at the bottom. Begin stitching in the strip section just above the first triangle leaving most of the strip section of the border free. Stitch all the way down to the bottom edge. Press the seams towards the centre of the quilt.

4 Pin the bottom border to the bottom edge of the quilt and this time stitch the full length of the border. Press seams as before.

5 Pin and stitch the righthand side border and the top border in the same way.

6 Finally stitch down the unsewn section of the lefthand side border and press seams.

7 Stitch the striped fabric top and bottom outer borders in place and press the seams away from the pieced borders.

MAKING THE PRAIRIE POINTS

1 This stage is best completed at the ironing board, have your scissors handy. To make the prairie points, place the lightweight fabric on the ironing board and press it in half lengthwise, then open it out again. Starting at the bottom right hand corner make a 45-degree fold so that the raw, side edge of the fabric meets the centre line, then press. Make a cut alongside the edge of the piece you have just folded, only cut as far as the centre line (diagram 4a).

diagram 4a

2 Continue in the same way until all the first stage folds on the lower half have been completed.

3 To complete the second stage, make a second fold so that the raw edges of each triangle meet the centre line, then press (diagram 4b).

diagram 4b

4 To make the points on the opposite edge you will need to offset the triangles. Turn the strip so that the unfolded edge is now nearest to you. Begin by trimming away the first and last 2 in/5 cm of this section, then make the folds and cuts as before (diagram 4c).

diagram 4c

5 Next fold along the centre line and slot the triangles one inside the other. Press well and run a line of machine stitching close to the edge of the long (centre) fold to prevent the prairie points (triangles) from slipping out of place (diagram 4d).

diagram 4d

6 Position the strip of prairie points along the top edge of the quilt, placing the long fold edge of the strip on the top edge of the right side of the quilt. The points should be pointing towards the quilt, baste the strip in place. Stitch through all layers.

FINISHING

1 Place the backing fabric on a flat surface, right side uppermost, and use masking tape or pins to hold it in place. Carefully position the quilt top, wrong side up, on top of the backing. Make sure all layers are smooth and pin the edges together leaving the edge with prairie points, open. Stitch the three pinned edges together.

NOTE Be careful not to stitch across the points of the pieced triangles as this will spoil the look of the finished quilt.

2 When the stitching has been completed and with the quilt still inside out, place it on the wadding, working on a flat surface as before.

3 Pin carefully and stitch through all three layers using the initial stitching line as a guide. The top edge is still unstitched at this stage. Trim away any excess wadding and backing fabric and turn the quilt through to the right side.

4 Begin by quilting a few lines across the large rectangles using the check as a guide. Quilt around each rectangle, quilting "in-the-ditch". Continue quilting, around the edge of the triangles, then echo these triangle shapes on the solid sections of the borders. Treat the top and bottom borders in the same way but don't quilt the top border.

5 To make the coin dots shown in the photograph opposite, draw round a large and a medium sized cotton reel to make rough circles on the felt pieces. You will need a total of 60 large and 60 small coin dots of mixed colours.

6 Place a small circle on a large one varying the colours within each section. Working on one centre section at a time, position the coins dots in a regular pattern on the centre rectangles and pin them in place. It helps to place the work in a large quilting hoop if you have one.

7 Thread a large needle with a length of coton à broder. Take the needle through the centre of the coin dot from the front of the work to the back, then bring it back through to the front coming up through the coin dot again. Tie the ends in a reef knot and snip the threads leaving ends of approximately ½ in/1.5 cm. Continue in the same way until all four centre sections have been completed.

8 On the back of the quilt, turn in the unfinished edge, baste first, then slip stitch in place. The turned-in edge should just cover the stitching line of the prairie points and these points should now be standing proud of the top edge of the quilt.

9 To complete, finish the remaining quilting on the top border.

HISTORICAL NOTE
Coin dots were popular in Victorian times and also in later years. They were often sewn edge-to-edge and used to make "penny rugs", the name penny coming from the old, large penny coins used as templates. The "coins" could also be placed edge-to-edge and over-sewn onto a backing fabric, to provide a warm bed cover. If felt was not available, then coin dots were made from old clothing especially woollen items that had been well washed and felted with use.

NOTE Make sure that the corners are fully pushed out and gently roll the edges between the thumb and first finger so that you achieve a firm edge. At this stage it is worth basting around the stitched edges to hold the layers in position. Although the sides of the quilt have been stitched together you will need to baste or safety pin the layers to keep them from moving during the quilting stage. The top edge remains open until the quilting has been completed.

Batik Beauty

Designed by Sarah Wellfair

The batik fabrics used in this quilt were such beautiful patterns, that to cut them into smaller pieces would have lost the impact of the designs. I chose to alternate the plain batiks with the simple four-patch block to provide a contrast and to single out some of the vibrant colours.

Finished size: 42½ x 36½ in/108 x 93 cm

MATERIALS

Blocks: 6 fat or long quarters of different batik designs and colours. I used four green/turquoise designs plus an orange and a pink for accent colours.

Border: dark blue or other contrasting colour, 20 in/50 cm

Wadding: lightweight cotton, 1¼ yds x 45 in/ 1 m x 115 cm wide

Backing: coordinating batik, 1¼ yds x 45 in/ 1 m x 115 cm wide

Machine quilting thread: purple metallic

Binding: 20 in/50 cm

ALTERNATIVE COLOUR SCHEMES

1 For a child's room, a bright selection of children's prints and coordinating plaids; 2 This block uses the same fabric pattern but in three different colourways to give a bright, unified design; 3 The large squares are cut from a pretty butterfly print with four contrasting fabrics for the four-patch to give a really sunny design; 4 A selection of hand-dyed fabrics gives a soft and completely different look.

1

2

3

4

CUTTING

1 From each of the fat quarters, cut ten $3\frac{1}{2}$ in/9 cm squares, then cut a total of fifteen $6\frac{1}{2}$ in/16.5 cm squares from the remaining pieces.

2 From the border fabric, cut four strips, $3\frac{1}{2}$ in/9 cm deep across the width of the fabric.

3 From the binding fabric, cut four strips, 3 in/7.5 cm deep across the width of the fabric.

STITCHING

1 Sort the $3\frac{1}{2}$ in/9 cm squares into pairs of colours – you can vary the combination but you need two pairs the same for each four-patch block. Place one of each colour right sides together and pin and stitch taking a $\frac{1}{4}$ in/0.75 cm seam allowance. Repeat with the remaining squares. Press the seams towards the darker fabric. You should now have 30 pairs (diagram 1).

diagram 1

2 Take two matching pairs, place right sides together, reversing the colours, and pin carefully, matching centre seams. Stitch together with the usual seam allowance (diagram 2). Repeat to make 15 four-patch blocks.

3 Following the quilt assembly plan on page 118, lay out the four-patch blocks alternating with the plain blocks until you are satisfied with the arrangement – you should have five blocks across and six down.

diagram 2

NOTE If you press the seam allowances in opposite directions the centre should lock together.

4 Working on the two vertical rows on the lefthand side of the arrangement, chain-piece the blocks together in pairs (diagram 3). Cut, open out and press the seams towards the solid blocks, then replace in the correct positions in the quilt plan.

diagram 3

5 Repeat with vertical rows three and four.

6 Pin and stitch the units together in horizontal rows, adding the single block from column five at the end of each row (diagram 4), then pin and stitch the horizontal rows together, being careful to match the seams. Press the seams towards the top row. The quilt should now measure approximately $30\frac{1}{2}$ x $36\frac{1}{2}$ in/ 76.5 x 91.5 cm.

diagram 4

7 Measure the pieced top through the centre from side to side for an accurate measurement, then trim two of the border strips to this measurement. Stitch to the top and bottom of the quilt. Press towards the border.

8 Measure the pieced top through the centre from top to bottom, then trim the remaining two border strips to this measurement. Stitch to the sides and press towards the border.

FINISHING

1 Measure the patchwork top and give it a final pressing.

2 Cut the wadding and backing 2 in/5 cm bigger all round than the finished patchwork size.

3 Spread the backing right side down on a flat surface, then smooth the wadding and the patchwork top, right side up, on top. Fasten together with safety pins or baste in a grid.

4 Machine quilt as desired. I have used a free motion quilting design with a heart motif using a purple metallic thread.

5 Trim the excess wadding and backing level with the patchwork top.

6 Cut the binding fabric into strips, 3 in/7.5 cm deep across the width of fabric. Fold in half lengthwise, wrong sides together and press.

7 Measure the quilt through the centre from top to bottom and cut two of the binding strips to this length. Pin one strip to the side of the quilt, matching raw edges. Stitch approximately $\frac{1}{2}$ in/1.5 cm in from the edge. Fold over to the back of the quilt and slip stitch down. Do the same on the opposite side of the quilt with the remaining strip.

8 Measure the quilt through the centre from side to side and add $1\frac{1}{2}$ in/4 cm to this for turnings. Cut two more binding strips to this length. Stitch to the top and bottom of the quilt, turning in a short hem at either end before folding to the back.

Blooming Borders

Designed by Sharon Chambers

It's summertime and the herbaceous borders are bursting with beautiful blooms. Take time to enjoy them with lunch on the lawn seated round this charming quilt. The design is so quick and easy you'll be delighted with how fast it grows! Make one as a gift in the lucky recipient's favourite flower shades and present it tucked inside a picnic basket.

Finished size: 54 x 42 in/135 x 105 cm

All fabrics used in the quilt top are 45 in/115 cm wide, 100% cotton.

Main fabric A for centre rectangle and outer borders: 55 in/1.4 m

Fabric B for first and third narrow borders: 24 in/60 cm

Fabric C for second narrow border: 15 in/40 cm

Fabric marker

Binding: striped fabric, 20 in/50 cm

Backing: 45 x 56 in/115 x 150 cm

Wadding: 100% cotton, 45 x 56 in/115 x 150 cm

Cotton quilting thread: to match or tone with top

ALTERNATIVE COLOUR SCHEMES

Roses were the inspiration behind the original quilt but you could equally well choose different flowers for your colour scheme. 1 These bright blues and yellows come from a border of forget-me-nots and tulips; 2 The small flower print is matched with a soft check and calico reminiscent of a cottage garden; 3 The reds, rusts and golds are a reminder of the stunning shades of autumn; 4 This final colour scheme is chosen to match a blue and white set of china.

1

2

3

4

CUTTING

1 From the main fabric **A**, cut four strips across the width of the fabric, 6½ in/16.5 cm deep. Cut these strips down to 42½ in/106.5 cm long. Set aside.

> **NOTE**
> To cut longer than the length of your ruler, fold the strip in half and cut half the finished length.

2 From the remainder of fabric **A**, cut a centre rectangle, 18½ x 30½ in/46.5 x 76.5 cm.

3 From fabric **B**, cut eight strips across the width of the fabric, 2½ in/6.5 cm deep. Trim two of these strips to 22½ in/56.5 cm long, four strips to 30½ in/76.5 cm long, and the remaining two strips to 38½ in/96.5 cm long. Set aside.

4 From fabric **C**, cut four strips across the width of the fabric, 2½ in/6.5 cm deep. Trim two of these strips to 26½ in/66.5 cm long and two to 34½ in/86.5 cm long. Set aside.

5 For the binding, lay the striped fabric out flat. Starting in the lower lefthand corner make the first diagonal cut on the true 45 degree bias of the fabric. Discard the corner triangle. Measuring from the diagonal edge of the fabric, cut eight strips 1½ in/4 cm wide (diagram 1). Be careful not to stretch these strips. Set aside.

diagram 1

STITCHING

1 Taking the usual ¼ in/0.75 cm seam, pin and stitch one of the 30½ in/76.5 cm border strips cut from fabric **B** to one of the long sides of the centre rectangle (diagram 2a). Repeat for the opposite side (diagram 2b). Press the seams towards the border strips. Pin and stitch one of the 22½ in/56.5 cm strips of fabric **B** to the top of the centre rectangle (diagram 2c) and repeat for the bottom of the rectangle (diagram 2d). Press the seams as before.

diagram 2a

diagram 2b

diagram 2c

diagram 2d

2 Pin and stitch the two 34½ in/86.5 cm long strips cut from fabric **C** to the sides of the rectangular panel pressing the seams as before. Stitch the 26½ in/66.5 cm strips of fabric **C** to the top and bottom. Press the seams.

3 From the remaining narrow border strips cut from fabric **B**, stitch the 38½ in/96.5 cm long strips to the sides first, then the 30½ in/76.5 cm strips to the top and bottom, pressing as usual.

4 Lastly, stitch the 6½ in/16.5 cm deep borders of fabric **A** to the sides, top and bottom, pressing as usual.

NOTE

To make sure you don't stretch the borders out of shape while stitching them, mark and pin the centre, the quarter points and both ends.

FINISHING

1 Mark the quilting lines as shown in diagram 3 on the finished top using an appropriate marker for the colour of your fabrics. The simple straight quilting lines made up of concentric 2 in/5 cm wide rectangles echo the size and shape of the narrow borders.

diagram 3

2 Measure the patchwork top and cut the wadding and backing fabric at least 1 in/2.5 cm larger all around.

3 Spread the backing right side down on a flat surface, then smooth the wadding and the patchwork top, right side up, on top. Fasten together with safety pins.

4 Using a walking foot, machine quilt through all three layers. Still with the walking foot attached, stitch a line of stay-stitching around the outside of the quilt ¼ in/0.75 cm in from the edge to stabilize it.

5 Join the binding strips with diagonal seams to make a continuous length to fit all round the quilt and use to bind the edges with a single-fold binding, mitred at the corners.

Candy Bars

Designed by Jean Hunt

Hot pink fabric frames the colourful bars in this topper for a single bed. Very simple blocks are joined together in rows to make the bars, reminiscent of the most colourful jars in the sweet shop. Simple quilting completes the project, which took just twelve hours to make.

Finished size: 59 x 47 in/150 x 120 cm

MATERIALS

All fabrics used in the quilt top are 45 in/115 cm wide, 100% cotton.

For the centre bars: 6½ in/17 cm of at least nine different small pattern or cloudy fabrics in pinks, oranges and mauves. These should be of approximately the same value, i.e. light or medium and preferably not too dark.

For the border and the plain bars: hot pink, 60 in/153 cm. This should be darker than the fabric for the "candy" coloured bars.

Binding: pink pattern, 7½ in/20 cm

Backing: size cotton or sheeting, 63 x 51 in/ 160 x 130 cm

Wadding: 2 oz polyester wadding or a cotton alternative, 63 x 51 in/160 x 130 cm

Machine quilting thread: to match, preferably cotton

ALTERNATIVE COLOUR SCHEMES

1 Dark centre strips with a light border reverses the colour scheme making the bars more prominent; 2 The cream and gold combination is a sophisticated colourway; 3 Blues and greens make a cool alternative; 4 Different shades of denim make a good colour scheme for a teenager.

1

2

3

4

CUTTING

1 From the nine strips for the centre bars, remove the selvage, then cut 49 rectangles measuring 7 x 6½ in/18 x 16.5 cm.

2 From the hot pink fabric, cut four strips, 3½ in/9 cm deep and approximately 60 in/153 cm wide, and six strips, 2½ in/6.5 cm deep and approximately 43 in/109 cm wide.

> **NOTE** You may wish to cut the hot pink strips after construction of the bars, as measurements may vary slightly.

3 Cut the binding fabric into strips, 1½ in/4 cm deep across the width.

STITCHING

1 Take your pile of 49 rectangles to the cutting board. Choose two different colours. Take the first rectangle and place it on the cutting board right side up, with the longer edge to the top. Take the second rectangle and place it on top of the first rectangle, also right side up. Using a rotary ruler and cutter, cut at an angle (approximately 60 degrees) from part way along the bottom long edge to the top long edge of the rectangles (you can use the markings on your ruler if you have them), thus splitting the rectangles into two pieces (diagram 1).

diagram 1

2 Take the lefthand piece of the first fabric rectangle and place it next to the righthand piece of the second fabric rectangle to form the first block. Stitch together by placing the two halves right sides together, aligning the raw edges and stitching a ¼ in/0.75 cm seam. Line up the tops of the two halves as accurately as possible. Repeat with the remaining two pieces to make your second block. The block should measure 6½ x 6½ in/16.5 x 16.5 cm.

3 Continue as above until all 49 blocks have been completed. Varying the angle of cut slightly each time gives a more interesting look but be careful not to mix up the pieces when cut – pin together if not stitching straightaway. When complete, press lightly.

4 Sort the blocks out on the floor, in seven rows each with seven blocks, until you are happy with the placement. Number the blocks, so that they do not become muddled.

5 Following the quilt assembly diagram on page 130, rotate each block 90 degrees to its neighbour, then pin and stitch together in rows taking the usual seam allowance and press.

6 To add the sashing strips, place a strip of 2½ in/6.5 cm deep hot pink fabric along the top of the bottom strip of blocks, right sides together and aligning raw edges. Pin carefully (the patchwork strips will stretch more than the plain strips), then stitch (diagram 2). Press the seams towards the sashing.

diagram 2

7 Place the next strip of blocks along the top of the pink sashing strip, right sides together and aligning raw edges. Pin and stitch. Press.

8 Repeat steps 6 and 7 until the seven strips of blocks have been joined with sashing strips in between.

ADDING THE BORDERS

1 Measure the pieced top through the centre from side to side, then trim two of the 3½ in/9 cm deep hot pink strips to this measurement. Pin and stitch to the top and bottom of the quilt.

2 Measure the pieced top through the centre from top to bottom, then trim the remaining two hot pink strips to this measurement. Pin and stitch to the sides.

FINISHING

1 Spread the backing right side down on a flat surface, then smooth the wadding and the patchwork top, right side up, on top. Fasten together with safety pins or baste in a grid.

2 Using a walking foot and the decorative stitches on your sewing machine, ideally a scallop or wave pattern, machine quilt in lines down and across the quilt, as desired.

3 Trim off any excess wadding and backing, so that they are even with the pieced top. Join the binding strips with diagonal seams to make a continuous length to fit all round the quilt and use to bind the edges with a double-fold binding, mitred at the corners.

Checks and Flowers

Designed by Rita Whitehorn

This simple design is made from a combination of strips and rectangles, which are quickly stitched together to make a cheerful bed quilt. The white broderie anglaise echoes the floral design in the small prints and the colour scheme is brought together by the strips of plain fabrics in between. The broderie anglaise will need to be backed with a fine lawn or similar to stop the wadding coming through the holes.

Finished size: 78 x 60 in/198 x 153 cm

MATERIALS
All fabrics used in the patchwork top are
45 in/115 cm wide, 100% cotton.

For the large and small blocks: one fat quarter of six
different colours (**A**, **C**, **D**, **E**, **F** and **G**) (I used three
mainly blue and three mainly yellow) plus ½ yd/50 cm
of broderie anglaise (**B**)

For outer border and infill strips: yellow (**H**),
3 yds/2.75 m
For inner border and infill strips: dark blue (**I**),
¾ yd/70 cm. (An extra ½ yd/50 cm will be needed if
this is used as an unbroken colour for binding.)
For infill strips: white (**J**), ¼ yd/25 cm
Backing: coordinating colour, 4 yds/3.75 m
Wadding: 80% wool and 20% mixed fibres, one piece,
64 x 82 in/163 x 208 cm
For broderie anglaise backing: lawn or a lighter
fabric, ½ yd/50 cm

ALTERNATIVE COLOUR SCHEMES

1 Floral fabrics coordinated with a stripe and a solid fabric in pastels make a restful colour scheme; 2 To match a natural coloured decor, choose green, tan and mustard fabrics; 3 For a boy's bedroom, pick a sporty print and team with bold primaries; 4 The boldness of the striking black floral print is toned down by the more subtle colours in the strips without losing the overall impact of this colour scheme.

1

2

3

4

Before cutting fabrics it is best to make a plan of the quilt blocks.

Press all seams to the darkest fabric at all times otherwise they will show through a light fabric. Do not press seams open at any time, this weakens the seams.

If you wish to use a directional print for the large and small blocks, you'll need extra fabric.

CUTTING

1 From the seven fabrics for the large and small blocks, cut the following:

from **A**, three large rectangles, $11\frac{1}{2}$ x $8\frac{1}{2}$ in/ 29 x 21.5 cm, and two small rectangles, $4\frac{1}{2}$ x $8\frac{1}{2}$ in/ 11.5 x 21.5 cm;

from **B**, three large rectangles, $11\frac{1}{2}$ x $8\frac{1}{2}$ in/ 29 x 21.5 cm, and two small rectangles, $4\frac{1}{2}$ x $8\frac{1}{2}$ in/ 11.5 x 21.5 cm;

from **C**, three large rectangles, $11\frac{1}{2}$ x $8\frac{1}{2}$ in/ 29 x 21.5 cm;

from **D**, three large rectangles, $11\frac{1}{2}$ x $8\frac{1}{2}$ in/ 29 x 21.5 cm;

from **E**, two large rectangles, $11\frac{1}{2}$ x $8\frac{1}{2}$ in/ 29 x 21.5 cm;

from **F**, two large rectangles, $11\frac{1}{2}$ x $8\frac{1}{2}$ in/ 29 x 21.5 cm;

from **G**, two large rectangles, $11\frac{1}{2}$ x $8\frac{1}{2}$ in/ 29 x 21.5 cm.

2 From the lawn backing fabric, cut three large rectangles, $11\frac{1}{2}$ x $8\frac{1}{2}$ in/29 x 21.5 cm, and two small rectangles, $4\frac{1}{2}$ x $8\frac{1}{2}$ in/11.5 x 21.5 cm.

3 From each of the yellow, dark blue and white fabrics (**H, I, J**) cut four strips across the width, 2 in/5 cm deep, for the infill strips.

STITCHING

1 Take one each of the yellow, white and dark blue 2 in/5 cm strips and seam together along the long edges. Press the seams away from the white fabric (diagram 1).

diagram 1

2 Repeat with the remaining three strips in each colour. Cross-cut these three-colour strips into rectangles, $8\frac{1}{2}$ in/21.5 cm wide (diagram 2). This should yield five rectangles from each of the four sets of three strips: 17 rectangles are required for the quilt.

diagram 2

3 Place the lawn backing fabric on the back of each of the broderie anglaise rectangles and tack together.

4 Following the quilt assembly plan on page 136, lay out the large and small rectangles in columns with infill strips in between.

5 Pin and stitch the blocks and infill strips together in columns, then pin and stitch the columns together. Remember to press all seams to darker fabrics.

ADDING THE BORDERS

1 For the inner border, measure the pieced top through the centre from side to side, then cut two strips to this measurement and 3 in/7.5 cm deep from the remaining dark blue fabric (**I**). Stitch to the top and bottom of the quilt.

2 Measure the pieced top through the centre from top to bottom, then cut four strips, 3 in/7.5 cm deep, from the remaining dark blue fabric. Join as necessary to make the required measurement. Pin and stitch to the sides.

3 For the outer border, measure the pieced top through the centre from side to side, then cut two strips to this measurement and 8 in/20 cm deep across the width of the remaining yellow fabric (**H**). Pin and stitch to the top and bottom of the quilt.

4 Measure the pieced top through the centre from top to bottom, then cut two strips, 8 in/20 cm deep, down the length of the remaining yellow fabric. Join as necessary to make the required measurement. Pin and stitch to the sides.

FINISHING

1 Measure the completed patchwork top and cut the backing fabric 2 in/5 cm bigger on all four sides. You may need to cut and join the backing fabric to fit.

NOTE Before joining the pieces of backing fabric, cut off the selvage edge, as this does not have any "give" and will create a taut seam. It is always best to cut off any selvage edge before joining any fabrics for that reason.

2 Spread the backing right side down on a flat surface, then smooth the wadding and the patchwork top, right side up, on top. Fasten together with safety pins or baste in a grid.

3 Machine or hand-quilt two vertical lines down each of the large rectangles and quilt in-the-ditch along the infill strips.

4 For the binding in a continuous dark blue (**I**), cut seven strips, 3 in/7.5 cm deep, across the width of the fabric. Cut one strip in half and join each portion to one whole length. Join two of the remaining strips into one whole length and repeat with the final two strips. Use to bind the edges with a double-fold binding, butted up at the corners.

5 Alternatively, to make a random fabric binding as shown in the photograph, you will need to cut strips of fabric from each of the blue fabrics, all 3 in/7.5 cm deep. Join with straight, not diagonal, seams to make four lengths to fit the four sides of the quilt and use as above.

Crosses and Squares

Designed by Katharine Guerrier

The accent is on economy both in time and expense for this quilt. The squares cut for the blocks are designed to make the best use of the fabric width and quick piecing techniques ensure that the blocks grow quickly. I pieced the backing from a "collage" of fabric pieces and blocks left over from other projects but I've given the measurements for using a single piece of fabric in the instructions. The quilting was done on a longarm quilting machine by Jan Chandler.

Finished size: 89 x 68 in/226 x 175 cm

MATERIALS
All fabrics used in the patchwork top are
45 in/115 cm wide, 100% cotton.

Green flower print and blue: 1¾ yds/1.5 m of each
For the sashing and borders: mauve, 2¼ yds/2 m
**For the sashing corner posts, corner rectangles and
binding:** orange, 1 yd/75 cm
Wadding: 2 oz or low loft, 72 x 93 in/185 x 236 cm
Backing: cotton, 72 x 93 in/185 x 236 cm

ALTERNATIVE COLOUR SCHEMES

1 Prints in bright colours and black would make an eye catching quilt for a modern interior; 2 Simple block designs like this will complement a collection of hand-dyed fabrics; 3 Use vintage floral print fabrics teamed with calico for an old-fashioned quilt with nostalgic appeal; 4 The natural colours of earth, sand and rock inspired this combination of colours.

1

2

3

4

CUTTING

1 From the green flower print fabric and the blue fabric, cut ten 14 in/35.5 cm squares each.

> **NOTE**
>
> You may find it easier to cut one set of squares to the exact size, then cut the partners slightly bigger, place the pairs right sides together with the accurately cut one on top, press, then mark and stitch. Now trim the larger squares to size. This will prevent the tendency that these large squares have to skew sideways making them difficult to fit.

2 From the mauve fabric, cut two strips down the length of the fabric, 10 x 57 in/25.5 x 145 cm wide for the top and bottom borders and two strips, 8 x 72 in/20.5 x 183 cm wide for the side borders.

3 From the mauve fabric, cut ten strips 2½ in/6.5 cm deep across the width and down the length of the remaining fabric, then sub-cut into 31 rectangles, 13½ in/34.5 cm long for the sashing strips.

4 From the orange fabric, cut one strip, 2½ in/6.5 cm deep, across the width of the fabric, then sub-cut into twelve squares for the "corner posts", i.e. the squares between the sashing strips.

5 From the orange fabric, cut one strip, 8 in/20.5 cm deep across the width of the fabric, then sub-cut into four rectangles 10 in/25.5 cm long for the corner rectangles.

6 From the remaining orange fabric, cut strips, 2½ in/ 6.5 cm deep of sufficient length to go around the outer edges of the quilt for the binding.

STITCHING

1 Place the ten green and blue squares in pairs, right sides together. Draw two diagonal lines on the top fabric of each pair, then pin and stitch ¼ in/0.75 cm away from the marked lines in the pattern illustrated (diagram 1). Trim both squares level if one square was cut larger.

diagram 1

2 Cut across both marked diagonals on each pair, then open out and pin stitch two of the resulting bi-coloured triangles together to make one block (diagram 2). Repeat to make twenty blocks.

diagram 2

3 Measure the blocks and check that they are 13½ in/34.5 cm square. If they are larger, trim to size. If they are smaller, trim all to the same size and trim the orange sashing strips to match.

4 Following the quilt assembly plan on page 142, stitch four rows of five blocks with a sashing strip between each. Press the seams towards the blocks.

5 Now pin and stitch three rows of sashing strips together with a corner post between each attached to the short side of the sashing strips. Press seams towards corner posts.

6 Pin and stitch the four rows of blocks together with a long sashing strip between each one matching points at intersecting corner post squares

ADDING THE BORDERS

1 Measure the patchwork top from top to bottom through the centre and trim two of the mauve border strips to this measurement for the sides. Next measure the patchwork top from side to side through the centre and trim the remaining two borders to this measurement for the top and bottom.

2 Pin and stitch the side borders to the patchwork top.

3 Pin and stitch one orange corner rectangle to each end of the two top and bottom mauve border strips, then pin and stitch to the top and bottom of the patchwork top (diagram 3).

diagram 3

FINISHING

1 Spread the backing right side down on a flat surface, then smooth the wadding and the patchwork top, right side up, on top. Fasten together with safety pins or baste in a grid.

2 Using the "free motion machine quilting" method and referring to the photograph as a guide, quilt over the surface. The quilt featured here was quilted on a longarm quilting machine in the "Floral Meander" pattern.

3 Trim the backing and wadding level with the edges of the quilt.

4 Join the binding strips with diagonal seams to make a continuous length to fit all round the quilt and use to bind the edges with a double-fold binding, mitred at the corners.

Sawtooth Fence

Designed by Katharine Guerrier

A strip of sawtooth triangles along the edges of these simple "Rail Fence" blocks give a contemporary look to this traditional favourite. The centre panel of sixteen blocks is framed in a border which uses more of the sawtooth triangles. The quilt is made in bright primary colours and uses quick piecing techniques for rapid results. The quilting was done on a longarm quilting machine by Jan Chandler.

Finished size: 55 in/140 cm square

MATERIALS
All fabrics used in the patchwork top are 45 in/115 cm wide, 100% cotton.

For the blocks and borders: 1 yd/1 m each in the following colours: red, yellow, blue and green
Binding: purple, 20 in/50 cm
Wadding: 2 oz or low loft, 60 x 60 in/ 152.5 x 152.5 cm
Backing: 100% cotton, 60 x 60 in/152.5 x 152.5 cm

ALTERNATIVE COLOUR SCHEMES

1 A combination of plaids and stripes will give a homespun effect; 2 Plain colours used together create an Amish-style quilt which will show off the quilting pattern well; 3 Blues teamed with a crisp white are popular in many other forms of decorative art such as Willow Pattern china and Delft floor tiles; 4 Earth colours will give a country feel to the quilt making a homely accent in any interior.

1

2

3

4

CUTTING

1 Remove the selvages from the red and yellow fabrics, then, cutting down the length of the fabric, cut eight strips, 5 in/12.5 cm wide from each colour.

2 Cut seven strips, 4 in/10 cm deep across the width of both the green and blue fabrics.

3 From the purple binding fabric, cut strips, $2\frac{1}{2}$ in/6.25 cm deep across the width of the fabric of sufficient length to go around the outer edges of the quilt.

STITCHING

1 Place one red and one yellow strip right sides together and stitch along the long edges taking a $\frac{1}{4}$ in/0.75 cm seam allowance. Press the seams to one side (diagram 1). Repeat with the other seven red and yellow strips.

diagram 1

2 Place one blue and one green strip right sides together and mark off 4 in/10 cm squares, then mark diagonal lines across the squares in a zigzag pattern. Stitch in a zigzag pattern $\frac{1}{4}$ in/0.75 cm away from both sides of the diagonal lines (diagram 2). Cut on the marked vertical and diagonal lines. Open out and press the seams to one side.

diagram 2

3 Repeat with the remaining blue and green strips to make a total of 64 half-square triangle units. Trim each of these bi-coloured squares to exactly $3\frac{1}{2}$ in/9 cm, checking that the seam still cuts across the diagonal.

4 Pin and stitch these bi-coloured squares together in sets of four to make a sawtooth strip (diagram 3).

diagram 3

ASSEMBLING THE BLOCKS

1 Place one of the sawtooth strips on top of the red/yellow strip, right sides together with the blue fabric against the red. Trim the red/yellow strip level with the sawtooth strip and repeat across the length of the strips, so that you have 16 yellow/red rectangles which are the same length as the sawtooth strips.

2 Pin and stitch the sawtooth strips to the red/yellow rectangles and press (diagram 4). You should have sixteen blocks.

diagram 4

3 Following the quilt assembly diagram on page 148, arrange the blocks in four rows of four blocks each to make the stepped design. Pin and stitch the blocks together in four rows, then stitch the rows together.

ADDING THE BORDERS

1 Using the same technique as described in step 2 of "Stitching", make a further 68 bi-coloured squares for the border. Stitch these together into two strips of seventeen squares for the bottom and lefthand side of the centre panel, one strip of sixteen squares for the top and one strip of eighteen squares for the right-hand side, checking the quilt assembly diagram for the correct orientation of the seams.

2 Stitch the strip of sixteen squares to the top of the panel, then stitch one of the strips of seventeen squares to the lefthand side. Next stitch the second strip of seventeen squares to the bottom and finally the strip of eighteen squares to the righthand side.

FINISHING

1 Spread the backing right side down on a flat surface, then smooth the wadding and the patchwork top, right side up, on top. Fasten together with safety pins or baste in a grid.

2 Using the "free motion machine quilting" method and referring to the photograph as a guide, machine quilt over the surface. The quilt featured here was quilted on a longarm quilting machine in the "Celtic Scroll" pattern.

3 Trim the backing and wadding level with the edges of the quilt. Join the binding strips with diagonal seams to make a continuous length to fit all round the quilt and use to bind the edges with a double-fold binding, mitred at the corners.

Whirligig Quilt

Designed by Dorothy Wood

The success of this quilt depends on accurate cutting and stitching. The plain colour fabrics can be layered together and cut all at once with a rotary cutter but it is advisable to cut the square pattern fabric in a single layer so that you can see exactly where you are cutting. Depending on the number of plain colours you use, you can create different patterns. Arrange the different colours randomly or in a simple pattern like the diagonal stripes used here.

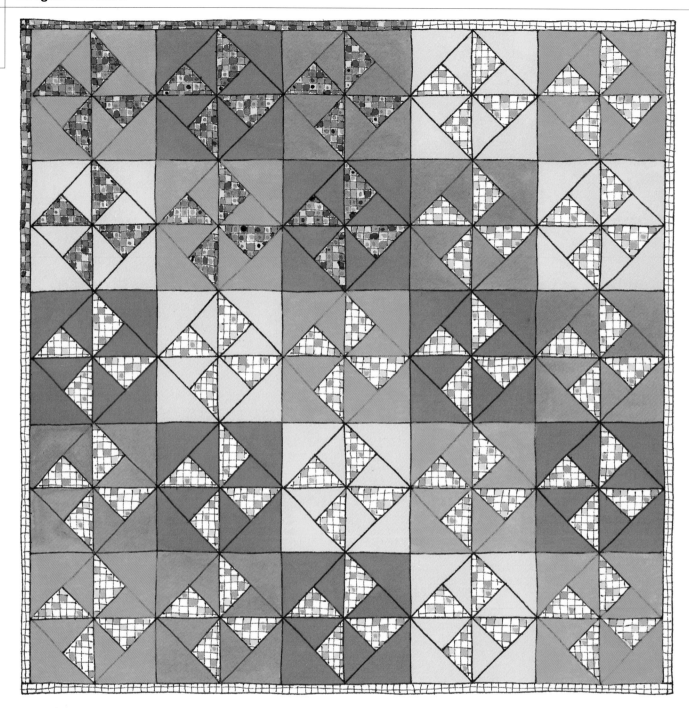

Finished size: 40 x 40 in /102 x 102 cm

MATERIALS

All fabrics used in the patchwork top are
45 in/115 cm wide, 100% cotton.
The backing fabric used is 45in/115cm wide.

Square print: 27 in/70 cm
Yellow, green, fuchsia and orange: 24 in/60 cm each
Backing: 42 x 42 in/107 x 107 cm
Wadding: low loft, 42 x 42 in/107 x 107 cm
White sewing thread
Dark blue stranded cotton
Needle

ALTERNATIVE COLOUR SCHEMES

1 By stitching the squares together in a slightly different way, you can create a second whirligig pattern; 2 With subtle shades such as this blue and cream check, try to match the creams exactly so that the two fabrics merge together; 3 Choose soft shades of background fabric to coordinate with the subtle stripes; 4 Pink and red are a fun combination. The contrasting patterns work because the pinks and reds are exactly the same colour – from the same fabric range.

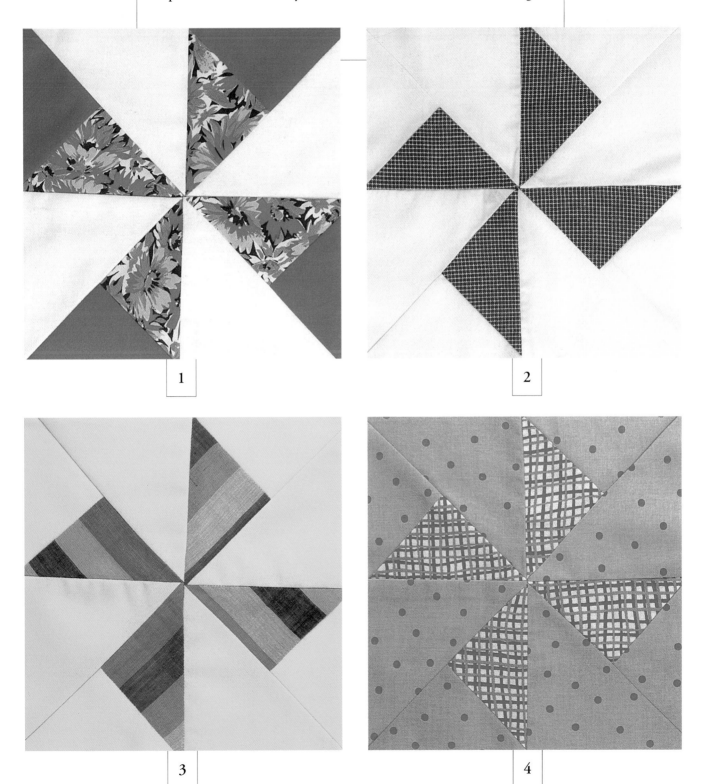

CUTTING

1 From the square print, cut four strips, $3^3/_4$ in/ 9.5 cm deep, across the width of the fabric, then cross-cut into fifty $3^3/_4$ in/9.5 cm squares. Cut the squares in half diagonally. Cut four strips, $2^3/_8$ x 42 in/ 6 x 106 cm deep, across the width for the binding.

2 Layer the coloured fabrics one on top of the other and steam press. Lay on the cutting mat. Cut ten $4^7/_8$ in/12.5 cm squares and five $5^1/_4$ in/13.5 cm squares from all of the colours.

3 Separate the layers and cut four more $4^7/_8$ in/ 12.5 cm squares from the fuchsia and the orange and two more from the yellow. Then cut one more $5^1/_4$ in/13.5 cm square in yellow and another two in orange and fuchsia.

4 Cut each of the solid coloured $4^7/_8$ in/12.5 cm squares in half diagonally. Cut each of the solid coloured $5^1/_4$ in/13.5 cm squares in half diagonally in both directions to make four quarters.

NOTE Follow the directions for pressing the seams carefully so that the seams face in opposite directions when pieces are joined together.

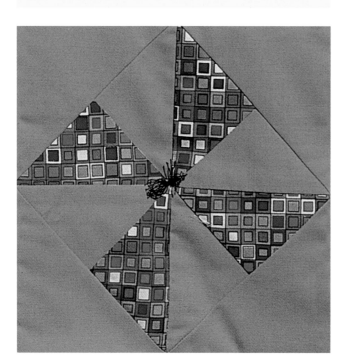

STITCHING

1 Take four smaller fuchsia triangles and four square print triangles. Arrange as shown in diagram 1.

diagram 1

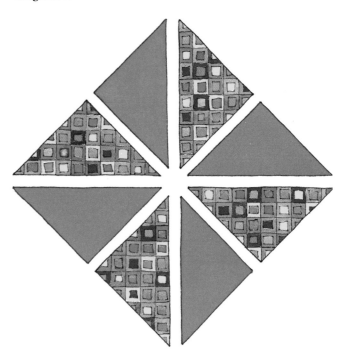

2 Stitch the four square print triangles to the fuchsia triangles taking a $1/_4$ in/0.75 cm seam to make four larger triangles and press the seams towards the pattern fabric (diagram 2).

diagram 2

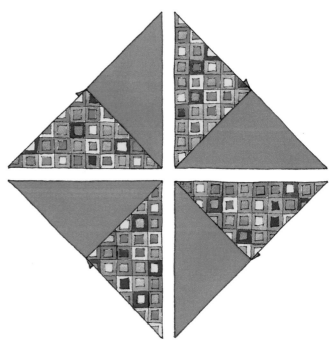

3 Stitch each of the joined triangles to a larger fuchsia triangle along the long edge with the usual seam allowance and press the seam towards the plain coloured fabric (diagram 3).

diagram 3

4 Arrange the squares to create the whirligig pattern. Pin the top two squares right sides together and stitch with a ¼ in/0.75 cm seam. Press the seam towards the fuchsia fabric. Stitch the bottom two squares together in the same way. Pin and stitch the two units together to finish the block and press the seam to one side.

5 Make all the square blocks in the same way with the remaining fuchsia triangles and the yellow, green and orange triangles, making sure that you press all the seams in the same way as the first block.

6 Following the quilt assembly diagram on page 154, lay out the blocks to form the pattern, with five squares in each of five rows. Check that the seams are all lying vertically. Alternate the direction of the seams in each row by turning the blocks round so that the first row seams face to the left and the next row faces to the right and so on. Pin and stitch the blocks together in rows.

7 Pin the first two rows together matching the seams carefully and stitch with a ¼ in/0.75 cm seam. Press the seam downwards.

8 Keep adding the rows one at a time until the patchwork top is complete.

FINISHING

1 Spread the backing right side down on a flat surface, then smooth out the wadding and the patchwork top, right side up, on top. Fasten together with safety pins or baste in a grid.

2 Trim the wadding and backing fabric to ½ in/ 1.5 cm away from the edge of the patchwork top using a rotary cutter.

3 Pin one of the binding strips down the side of the quilt, right sides together, so that the raw edges are aligned. Stitch with the usual seam allowance.

4 Fold the binding strip to the reverse of the quilt, turn under a ¼ in/0.75 cm hem and slip stitch to the backing fabric. Trim the ends level with the wadding. Repeat to add a binding strip to the opposite side.

5 Pin the remaining two binding strips to the top and bottom of the quilt. Machine stitch as before. Trim the ends of the binding to extend only ¼ in/0.75 cm beyond the quilt, then turn under level with the edge of the quilt top before folding over and stitching to the reverse side as before.

6 Slip stitch the corners of the binding neatly.

7 Turn the quilt so that the right side is facing up. To tie the quilt, cut a length of stranded cotton and thread onto a needle. Take a small stitch in the centre of the first whirligig block and pull the thread through leaving a 2 in/5 cm tail. Make a little back stitch and pull the thread through again. Trim to 2 in/5 cm.

8 Stitch a second thread through the centre of the whirligig and tie the ends in a reef (square) knot. Trim all thread ends to ½ in /1.5 cm.

A Kiss and A Cuddle

Designed by Sharon Chambers

This oh-so-simple lap quilt made from nostalgic 1930s reproduction fabrics and natural calico is just the thing to warm the heart of someone special. It's the perfect size to cuddle up underneath and there's a kiss sewn right into the middle of it.

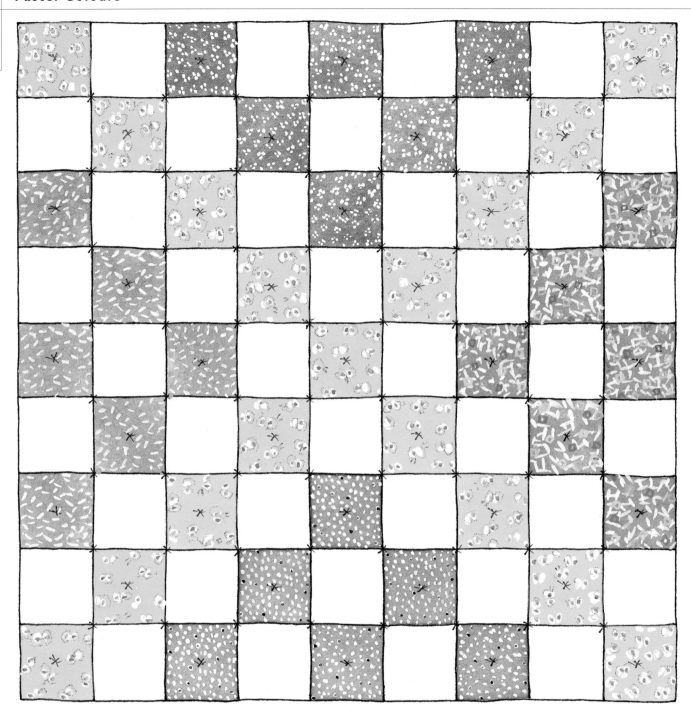

Finished size: 54 x 54 in/135 x 135 cm

MATERIALS
All fabrics used in the quilt top are 45 in/115 cm
wide, 100% cotton.

Main patterned fabric for centre "kiss": ⅔ yd/60 cm
Four co-ordinating patterned fabrics: ¼ yd/25 cm of
each

Natural calico for alternate squares: 1½ yds/1.4 m
Backing: 3¼ yds/2.9 m
Wadding: 2 oz polyester, 56 x 56 in/140 x 140 cm
Needle: crewel or embroidery needle or a size three
betweens needle
Stranded embroidery cotton: one skein each of five
colours to match the five patterned fabrics
Coton à broder: one skein no. 16 to match the calico

ALTERNATIVE COLOUR SCHEMES

The simplicity of this quilt pattern adapts to so many different possibilities that you are spoilt for choice. Make it to match a granddaughter's bedroom or in the colours of a grandson's favourite football team. Light or dark, sharp or sweet, it all works. 1 Various pink prints with calico; 2 Red and black plains with calico; 3 Sharp rich colours with Madras plaid; 4 Novelty prints with yellow.

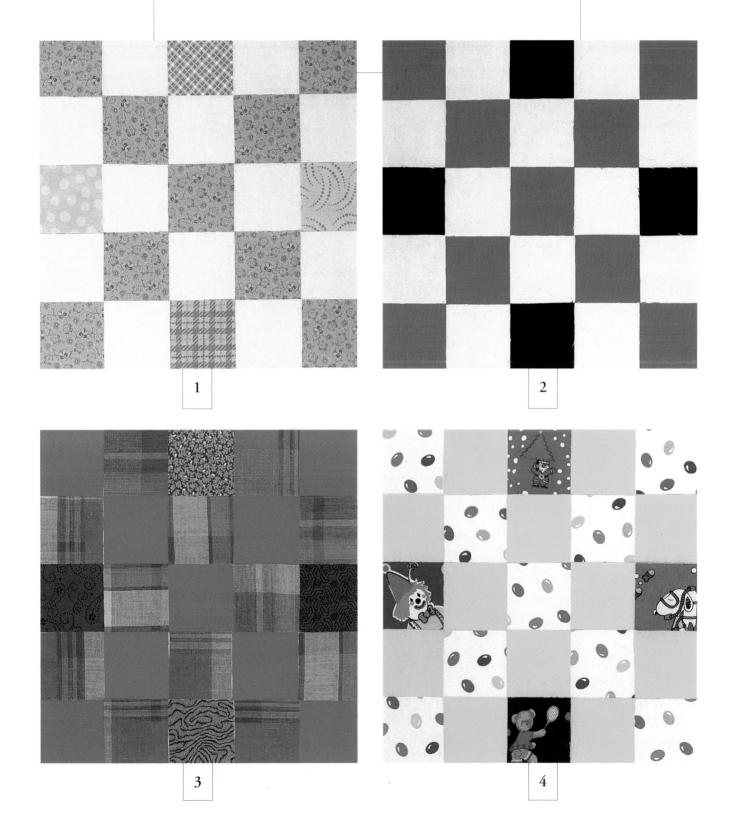

CUTTING

1 From the main patterned fabric, cut three strips, 6½ in/16.5 cm deep, across the width of the fabric. Cross-cut these strips into 6½ in/16.5 cm squares, avoiding the selvages. You should be able to get six squares from each strip, so you will have one left over.

2 From each of the four co-ordinating patterned fabrics, cut a strip 6½ in/16.5 cm deep across the width of the fabric. Cross-cut each strip into six 6½ in/16.5 cm squares avoiding the selvages.

3 From the calico, cut seven strips 6½ in/16.5 cm deep across the width of the fabric. Cross-cut these strips into 6½ in/16.5 cm squares avoiding the selvages. You need forty squares, so you will have two left over.

4 Cut the backing fabric into two lengths of 56 in/140 cm each.

STITCHING

1 Following the quilt assembly diagram on page 160, lay out all the fabric squares in their correct places. Stack up the squares for each row so that the first square on the left is at the top of the pile.

2 Beginning with row one and stitching with a ¼ in/0.75 cm seam allowance, stitch the squares together in four pairs (leaving the last square in the row unstitched for the moment).

NOTE Always stack in the same order and pin or tape an identifying letter or number to each row to help you keep the rows in sequence.

3 Stitch the pairs together into two strips of four squares, then stitch these two strips together. Finally, stitch the last square to the end of the row. Set the completed row aside.

4 Stitch the rest of the rows together in exactly the same way. Press all of the seams towards the patterned fabrics, so that when you stitch the rows together all the short seams will interlock making it easy to match up seam lines.

5 Pin and stitch the rows together. Press all the long seams in the same direction.

6 Trim the selvages from the backing fabric. With right sides together, seam the two lengths together down the long side, taking the usual seam allowance. Press the seam to one side.

FINISHING

NOTE The edges of this quilt are finished without a separate binding, before the tying and quilting are done.

1 Lay the patchwork top over the pieced backing fabric wrong sides together with the centre seam of the backing aligned with the middle of the patchwork top. Pin the two together to keep them from shifting. Trim off excess backing fabric even with the edges of the patchwork top (diagram 1). Unpin.

diagram 1

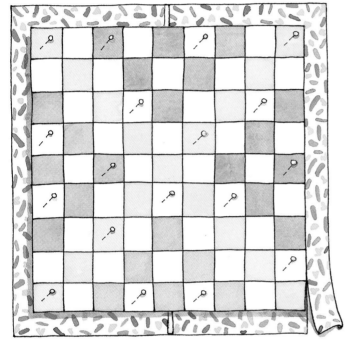

2 Spread out the wadding on a smooth flat surface making sure there are no wrinkles. Place the backing fabric on the wadding right side up. Place the quilt top over the backing, right side down and aligning all four edges evenly. Pin with straight pins around the edges to keep them from shifting. Stitch around all four sides with a $\frac{1}{4}$ in/0.75 cm seam allowance leaving an opening of about 15 – 18 in/35 – 45 cm on one side for turning. Carefully trim away excess wadding across the corners to reduce bulk when turning (diagram 2).

diagram 2

3 Turn quilt right side out, so that the wadding is now sandwiched between the backing and the patchwork top and slip-stitch the opening closed.

4 Smooth out the layers of the quilt rolling the edges and finger-pressing them so that the seam lies along the edge or just underneath. Pin safety pins along the edges and spaced out over the top to hold everything in place while tying and quilting.

5 Using three strands of embroidery floss, doubled but not knotted, tie as shown in diagram 3. Trim the ends after tying.

diagram 3

6 Mark the quilting pattern in the calico squares as shown in diagram 4 and, using a single strand of coton à broder thread, quilt in large naive style stitches. Finally, stitch a double row of stitches around the outside edge to give a neat finish to the quilt. If you have trouble pulling the knots through to the wadding, leave them on the outside or knot one end of the thread to the next. Remember, it's meant to be cuddly, not perfect!

diagram 4

Dotty Cot Quilt

Designed by Rita Whitehorn

This little cot quilt is best suited to a baby from the age of nine months upwards, when he or she can move round more freely and kick off the cover if it becomes too warm. Its mixture of soft pastel blues, pinks, greens and yellow will suit either a little boy or a little girl.

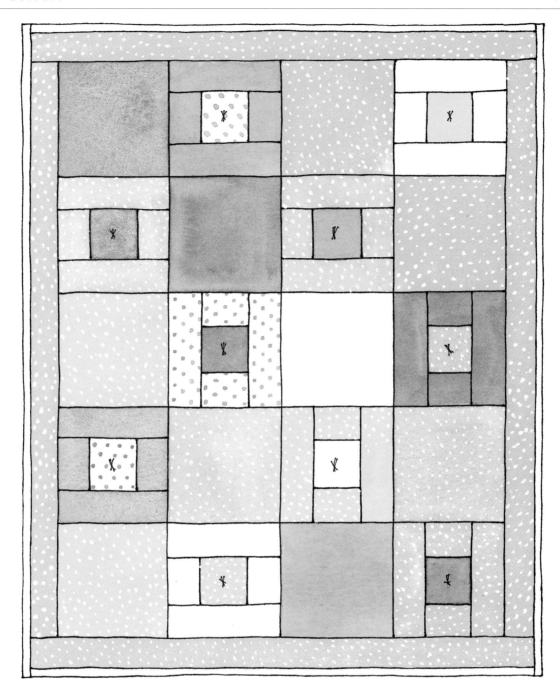

Finished size: 37 x 30 in/86 x 71 cm

MATERIALS
All fabrics used in the quilt top are 45 in/115 cm
wide, 100% cotton.

Print fabrics: 9 in/25 cm of each of seven colours. I
used pastel small flowery prints in yellow, green, pink
and blue, dotty prints in blue and white and pink and
white plus a white-on-white print
Plain fabrics: 9 in/25 cm of each of four colours. I
used pastels in shades of blue, pink, lilac and green to

match the prints
Binding: An extra ½ yd/50 cm of the white-on-white
print
Border: An extra ½ yd/50 cm of the green flowery
print
Wadding: 34 x 41 in/86 x 104 cm
Backing: 34 x 41 in/86 x 104 cm
Template plastic for circle
Marking pencil
Quilting thread
Stranded embroidery cotton or perle

ALTERNATIVE COLOUR SCHEMES

Each of these four alternative colourways is based on having a pretty baby's print in the centre of the pieced blocks. You could vary the colour of the borders round the print to add variety and pick out the background colour for the alternative plain blocks.

1

2

3

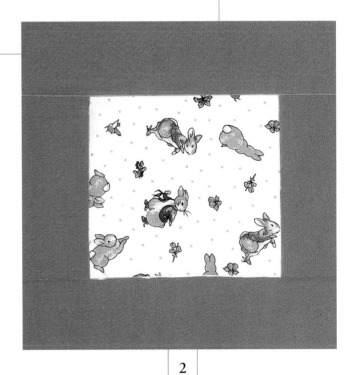

4

CUTTING

Follow the quilt assembly diagram on page 166 for the placement of the prints and plain fabrics. Alternatively, make your own colour plan before you start.

1 From each of the print and plain fabrics except the green print, cut one $3\frac{1}{4}$ x $3\frac{1}{4}$ in/8 x 8 cm square for the inner squares of the pieced blocks. You need a total of ten small squares.

2 From the print and plain fabrics, except the plain green, cut strips across the width of the fabric, $2\frac{1}{4}$ in/5.5 cm deep.

3 From the print and plain fabrics cut 10 squares, $6\frac{3}{4}$ x $6\frac{3}{4}$ in/16 x 16 cm to alternate with the pieced blocks. You could have a different fabric for each square but I chose not to use the stronger prints as they would be too dominant, so I cut one each of plain pink, plain blue and plain lilac; one each of pink print, white-on-white and blue print; and two each of green print and yellow print.

4 From the green flowery print, cut 4 strips $2\frac{1}{4}$ in/5.5 cm deep across the width of fabric for the borders.

5 From the white-on-white print, cut 4 strips of fabric 2 in/5 cm deep across the width of the fabric for the binding.

STITCHING

1 Following the quilt assembly diagram for the correct matching of fabrics, place one fabric strip right sides together with one small square, aligning raw edges. Stitch taking a $\frac{1}{4}$ in/0.75 cm seam allowance. Trim the strip level with the square (diagram 1).

diagram 1

2 Repeat to stitch the same strip to the bottom edge of the square and trim (diagram 2a). Press the seams to the darker fabric (diagram 2b).

diagram 2a   *diagram 2b*

3 Repeat as above to stitch a strip to the right side of the block (diagram 3a), then to the left (diagram 3b). This completes the "square within a square" block.

diagram 3a   *diagram 3b*

4 Still following the quilt assembly plan, stitch nine more blocks in the same way.

5 Lay out the blocks alternating with the larger plain squares in five rows of four squares.

6 Stitch the squares in each row together, taking a $\frac{1}{4}$ in/0.75 cm seam allowance, then pin and stitch the rows together, carefully matching seams.

ADDING THE BORDERS

1 Measure the pieced top through the centre from top to bottom, then trim two of the border strips to this measurement. Stitch to each side of the top.

2 Measure the pieced top through the centre from side to side, then trim two of the border strips to this measurement. Stitch to the top and bottom.

FINISHING

1 Spread the backing right side down on a flat surface, then smooth out the wadding and the patchwork top, right side up, on top. Fasten together with safety pins or baste in a grid.

2 Using the template plastic, make a template from the circle given below. Use the template and marking pencil to mark circles in the centre of each of the plain squares of the pieced top. Quilt round these circles by hand using large stitches.

3 To add ties to the quilt, lightly mark the centre of each inner square of the pieced blocks. Thread a large needle with the embroidery cotton or perlé and insert the needle ¼ in/0.75 cm to the right of the marked centre point, then bring needle out about

½ in/1.5 cm to the left of the entry point leaving a "tail" of thread about 3 in/7.5 cm long. Put needle back into first hole and come back up into the same place as first exit point and cut thread about 3 in/ 7.5 cm from this point. Tie a double knot but do not pull too tightly. Trim thread to length desired (diagram 4).

diagram 4

4 To bind the quilt, on each of the binding strips fold over ¼ in/0.75 cm of fabric to the wrong side of fabric and press.

5 Place right side of binding to right side of the quilt top, raw edges to raw edges, pin tack or baste, then stitch taking a ¼ in/0.75 cm seam allowance through all the layers. Trim off excess binding in line with the quilt top.

6 Fold over the binding to the wrong side of the quilt and slip stitch in place along the previously pressed up edge, using a matching thread to the binding fabric.

7 Repeat for the left side of the quilt. Add binding strips to the top and bottom in the same way but turn in a small hem at each end of the strip before folding to the back and hemstitching.

*Template
Actual size*

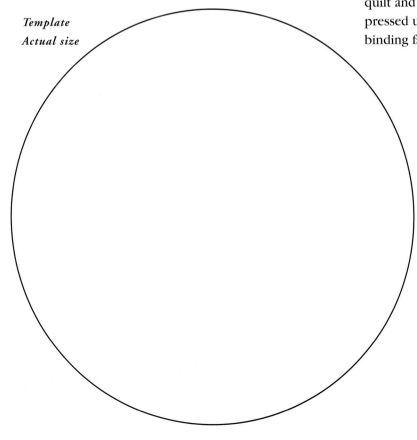

Friends at Heart

Designed by Nikki Foley

Colourful pastels and vibrant pink make this a beautiful single bed quilt, that any little girl (or big girl) would be delighted to receive as a gift. It was inspired by sweet peas in a cottage garden.

Finished quilt size 58½ x 43 in/149 x 109 cm

MATERIALS
All fabrics used in the quilt top are 45 in/115 cm wide, 100% cotton.

For the blocks: 14 in/35 cm of each of four fabrics – two pinks and two lilacs

For the inner border and hearts: vibrant pink, 28 in/71 cm

For the outer border: lilac/pink, 15 in/38 cm

Binding: lilac, 10 in/25 cm

Backing: 60 x 45 in/153 x 114 cm

Wadding: 60 x 45 in/153 x 114 cm

Machine quilting thread

Fusible webbing

ALTERNATIVE COLOUR SCHEMES

Keeping the colours soft and romantic to echo the heart motif, it's still possible to achieve a variety of different effects. 1 Strong purple hearts sit over lilac and cream prints; 2 A checked fabric for the hearts merges well with the floral pale pink and cream fabrics in the four-square blocks; 3 Orange hearts and warm yellows make a sunny colour scheme; 4 Strong toned pinks and lilacs produce an ultra-feminine design.

1

2

3

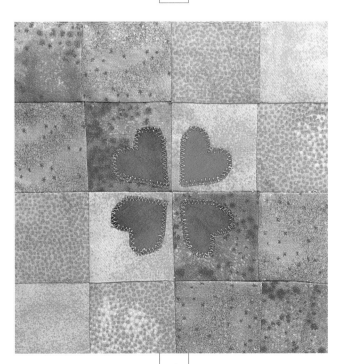

4

CUTTING

1 From the pink and lilac fabrics, first cut off the selvages, then cut into strips, $4\frac{1}{2}$ in/11.5 cm deep across the width. As you will be joining the two pink fabrics together and the two lilacs together, they will be referred to as pink **A** and pink **B** and lilac **A** and lilac **B**.

2 From the vibrant pink inner border fabric, cut five strips, $3\frac{1}{2}$ in/9 cm deep across the width, reserving the remainder for the hearts.

3 From the outer border fabric, cut strips, 3 in/7.5 cm deep across the width.

4 From the binding fabric, cut strips, 2 in/5 cm deep across the width.

5 Trace around the heart template given below onto the paper side of the fusible webbing 24 times. Carefully cut around each heart. Place the hearts, paper side up, onto the wrong side of the remaining vibrant pink fabric, then press with a fairly hot iron with the steam off. Cut the hearts out of the fabric leaving the paper backing on until you are ready to use them.

Template
Actual size

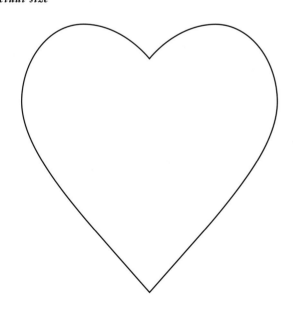

STITCHING

1 To make up the blocks, place a pink A strip right sides together with a pink B strip and stitch, taking a $\frac{1}{4}$ in/0.75 cm seam allowance. Press the seams to one side.

2 Stitch a lilac A strip to a lilac B strip in the same way.

3 Repeat with the remaining two strips of each colour, then cut each of these two-colour strips into $4\frac{1}{2}$ in/11.5 cm rectangles (diagram 1). You need a total of 24 in pink and 24 in lilac.

diagram 1

4 Starting with the pink units, place one rectangle on top of another right sides together but reversing the colours, so that pink A sits on top of pink B. Pin and stitch together to make a four-patch block (diagram 2).

diagram 2

5 Do the same with two lilac rectangles. Repeat to make four-square blocks from all of the remaining rectangles. You should now have 24 blocks altogether – 12 pink and 12 lilac. Press the seams to one side.

6 Following the quilt assembly diagram on page 172, lay out the blocks alternating pink and lilac in four columns each with six blocks.

7 Pin and stitch the blocks together in rows, then the rows together.

8 Position the hearts in groups of four on the patchwork as shown in diagram 3. When you are happy with the placement, remove the paper backing and iron in place. Take care that the hearts do not move out of place when ironing. Machine stitch around the edge of each heart with a zigzag stitch, using a matching thread.

diagram 3

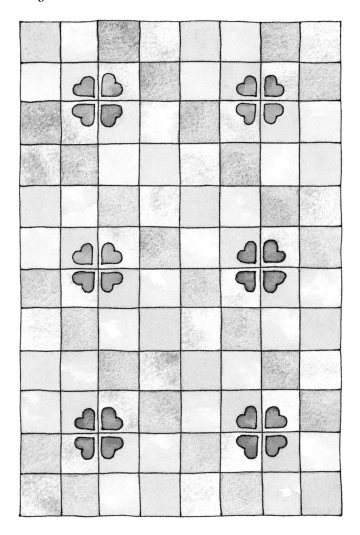

ADDING THE BORDERS

1 Measure the pieced top through the centre from side to side, then make two strips to this length from the vibrant pink inner border strips, joining if necessary. Stitch to the top and bottom of the quilt and press.

2 Measure the pieced top through the centre from top to bottom, then join strips of the vibrant pink inner border fabric to this measurement. Stitch to the sides and press.

3 Repeat the measuring and stitching process in steps 1 and 2 to attach the outer border fabric strips to the patchwork top and press.

FINISHING

1 Spread the backing right side down on a flat surface, then smooth the wadding and the patchwork top, right side up, on top. Fasten together with safety pins or baste in a grid.

2 Using a walking foot and decorative stitches, machine quilt as desired. The quilt in the photograph has been quilted with diagonal lines through the four-square blocks and a wavy design along the edges of the inner border.

3 Trim off any excess wadding and backing so they are even with the pieced top. Join the binding strips with diagonal seams to make a continuous length to fit all round the quilt and use to bind the edges with a double-fold binding, mitred at the corners.

NOTE If you don't do the zigzag stitching used to appliqué the hearts all in one go, make a note of the width and length of the stitch used. You may not remember what settings your machine was on next time you come to use it.

Noughts and Crosses

Designed by Sarah Wellfair

This is a simple but highly effective design made of "Rail Fence" blocks and half-square triangles. The similarity of the fabrics used gives an overall pattern to the quilt without emphasizing the patchwork pieces. This quilt could be made bigger by adding more blocks or even a wider border. The squares could be made from scraps to make every block a different colour scheme.

Finished size: 41 in/103 cm square

MATERIALS
All fabrics used in the quilt top are 45 in/115 cm wide, 100% cotton.

Main fabric for half square triangles, rail fence block and outer border: cream novelty print, **A**, 1⅜ yds/1.25 m

For half-square triangles: blue spot, **B**, 10 in/25 cm
For rail fence block: blue cloud pattern, **C**, 10 in/25 cm
For sashing, rail fence block and inner border: green spot, **D**, 20 in/50 cm
Backing: coordinating colour, 1¼ yds/1 m
Wadding: lightweight cotton or polyester, 1¼ yds/1 m
Binding: cream, 20 in/50 cm

ALTERNATIVE COLOUR SCHEMES

1 A selection of Christmas fabrics in traditional colours looks really festive; 2 A range of autumn reds, golds and purples makes a warm and comforting quilt; 3 A variety of different blue prints produces a harmonious colour scheme; 4 Fabrics with a check or a plaid pattern work well with matching floral fabrics interspersed with some plain.

1

2

3

4

CUTTING

1 From fabric **A,** cut the following:

two strips, $1\frac{7}{8}$ x 44 in/5 x 114 cm;

eight squares, $5\frac{1}{2}$ in/14.5 cm;

four squares, $4\frac{5}{8}$ in/12 cm;

one square, $2\frac{1}{2}$ in/6.5 cm;

two strips, $4\frac{1}{2}$ x $40\frac{1}{4}$ in/11.5 x 101 cm;

two strips, $4\frac{1}{2}$ x $31\frac{3}{4}$ in/11.5 x 79.5 cm.

2 From fabric **B,** cut eight squares, $5\frac{1}{2}$ in/14.5 cm.

3 From fabric **C,** cut two strips, $1\frac{7}{8}$ x 44 in/ 5 x 114 cm.

4 From fabric **D,** cut the following:

two strips, $1\frac{7}{8}$ x 44 in/5 x 114 cm;

four strips, $2\frac{1}{2}$ x $12\frac{7}{8}$ in/6.5 x 33 cm;

two strips, $2\frac{1}{2}$ x $27\frac{1}{4}$ in/6.5 x 68 cm;

two strips, $2\frac{1}{2}$ x $31\frac{3}{4}$ in/6.5 x 79.5 cm.

NOTE The block is made up of four half-square triangles, four rail fence blocks and one plain square. It will help with the assembly if you label each of the different fabrics A to D, as shown in diagram 1.

diagram 1

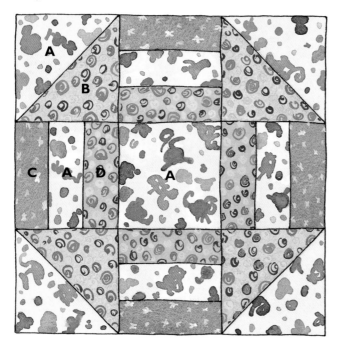

STITCHING

1 Take one $1\frac{7}{8}$ in/5 cm strip of **A** and one $1\frac{7}{8}$ in/ 5 cm strip of **C**, place right sides together and stitch down one long side taking a $\frac{1}{4}$ in/0.75 cm seam allowance. Do the same to the remaining two strips of the same colour.

2 Take the two **D** $1\frac{7}{8}$ in/5 cm wide strips and stitch to the other side of the cream strips with the same seam allowance. Press the seams towards the darker fabric.

3 The strips should now be approx $4\frac{5}{8}$ in/12 cm wide. Using a rotary cutter and ruler, cross-cut the strips into $4\frac{5}{8}$ in/12 cm squares – you will need 16 squares in total (diagram 2).

diagram 2

4 Take one **A** $5\frac{1}{2}$ in/14.5 cm square and place right sides together with one **B** $5\frac{1}{2}$ in/14.5 cm square. Repeat with the remaining seven **A** and **B** squares. With the cream fabric uppermost, pencil draw a line diagonally from corner to corner.

5 Stitch $\frac{1}{4}$ in/0.75 cm on either side of the marked line on all eight squares (diagram 3).

diagram 3

6 Cut squares in half along the marked line. Open and press the seams towards the darker fabric. You should now have 16 squares of half-square triangles.

7 Following the block layout in diagram 1, lay out the pieced squares. Taking the usual seam allowance, stitch together first in rows, then the rows together, being careful to match seams as you go. Stitch all four blocks the same way.

8 Take two of the 2½ x 12⅞ in/6.5 x 33 cm sashing strips, **D**, and stitch one 2½ in/6.5 cm square to the short end of one strip, then stitch the other sashing strip to the opposite side of the square. Press the seams towards the sashing strips (diagram 4).

diagram 4

9 Take the other two sashing strips and stitch one between each pair of blocks. Press the seams towards the sashing (diagram 5).

diagram 5

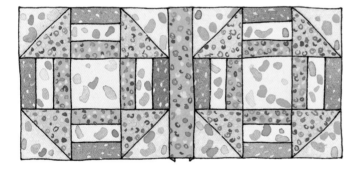

10 Stitch the sashing strip made in step 8 between the two units made in step 9.

ADDING THE BORDERS

1 Take two 27¼ in/68 cm inner border strips, **D**, and pin and stitch one to the top edge and one to the bottom edge of the patchwork.

2 Take the remaining two 31¾ in/79.5 cm inner border strips, **D**, and pin and stitch to the sides.

3 Take the two 31¾ in/79.5 cm outer border strips, **A**, and stitch to the top and bottom of quilt.

4 Take the remaining two 40¼ in/101 cm outer border strips, **A**, and stitch to the sides of the quilt.

FINISHING

1 Measure the patchwork top and give it a final pressing.

2 Cut the wadding and backing 2 in/5 cm bigger all round than the finished quilt size.

3 Spread the backing right side down on a flat surface, then smooth the wadding and the patchwork top, right side up, on top. Fasten together with safety pins or baste in a grid.

4 Machine quilt as desired. I have random quilted the centre and quilted free motion random hearts in the border.

5 Trim the excess wadding and backing level with the patchwork top.

6 Cut the binding fabric into 3 in/7.5 cm strips across width of fabric. Fold in half lengthwise and press.

7 Measure the quilt through the centre from top to bottom and cut two of the binding strips to this length. Pin one strip to the side of the quilt, matching raw edges. Stitch approximately ½ in/1.5 cm in from the edge. Fold over to the back of the quilt, turn under a hem and slip stitch down. Do the same on the opposite side of the quilt with the remaining strip.

8 Measure the quilt through the centre from side to side and add 1½ in/4 cm to this for turnings. Cut two more binding strips to this length. Stitch to the top and bottom of the quilt, turning in a short hem at either end before folding to the back, turning under a hem and slip stitching to the backing.

Pretty Pinwheels

Designed by Alison Wood

Although there are many different traditional quilt blocks which can be made from half square triangles such as these, the pinwheel is a simple and effective setting. Spacing the pinwheels with alternate plain squares gives an uncluttered look and for lovers of hand quilting there is plenty of scope for embellishment. The quilt could be made with treasured scraps or just two contrasting fabrics for a strong graphic look. The quilt shown uses 17 fabrics based on a collection of ten co-ordinating florals with the addition of some crisp ginghams and pastel marble fabrics. The width means that it can be inexpensively backed with 60 in/154 cm wide calico.

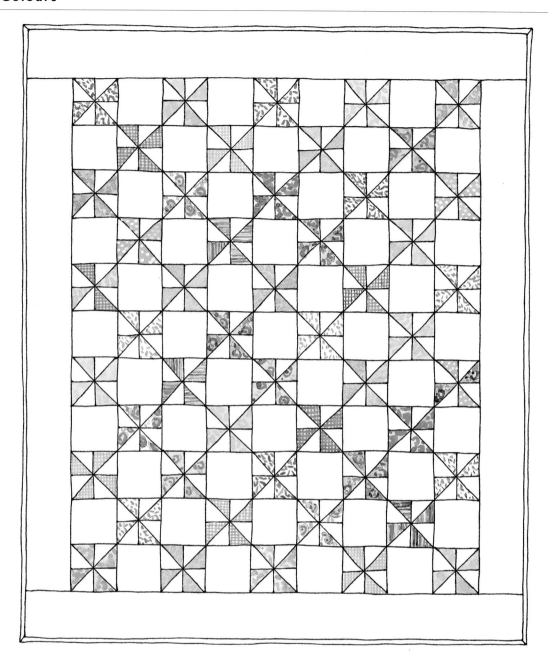

Finished size: 67 x 55 in/170 x 140 cm

MATERIALS
The white calico used in the quilt top is 60 in/154 cm wide. An alternative quantity is given for 45 in/115 cm wide background fabric.

Pinwheels: main fabric, ¾ yd/75 cm, 45 in/115 cm wide. If using scraps a minimum of two 3⅛ in/8 cm squares are needed for each pinwheel block and 100 squares are needed altogether. A fat eighth of a yard or metre should yield 18 x 3⅛ in/8 cm squares; a fat quarter should yield 36 squares.

Background pinwheel fabric: calico, ⅔ yd/60 cm, 60 in/154 cm wide OR ¾ yd/75 cm, 45 in/115 cm wide

Plain alternate squares: calico, ⅞ yd/75 cm, 60 in/154 cm wide OR 1 yd/1 m, 45 in/115 cm wide

Borders: calico, ⅔ yd/60 cm, 60 in/154 cm wide OR 1 yd/1 m, 45 in/115 cm wide

Binding: ½ yd/50 cm or use scraps

Backing: calico, 2 yds/2 m, 60 in/154 cm wide OR 4 yds/3.5 m, 45 in/115 cm wide fabric cut in half and joined with the seam running horizontally

Wadding: approx. 72 x 92 in/183 x 234 cm (twin or single size). Cotton or 80:20 cotton/polyester mix is more suitable for machine quilting. For hand quilting use either cotton/cotton blend or 2 oz polyester.

Medium lead pencil or quilt marking pencil

Hera marker (optional)

ALTERNATIVE COLOUR SCHEMES

1 Rainbow stripes and a purple print make an eyecatching contemporary design – make sure the stripes always run parallel to one of the seams; 2 The high contrast of indigo and white is highly effective; 3 Soft country floral and pastel polka dots make a restful quilt; 4 Plaids and dots in bright colours make a zingy colourway for a child's room.

1

2

3

4

CUTTING

1 From the fabric or fabrics chosen for the pin-wheels, cut strips $3\frac{1}{8}$ in/8 cm deep across the width. Cross-cut the strips into $3\frac{1}{8}$ in/8 cm squares. You will need 100 squares. Put these to one side.

2 From the background fabric, cut 100 x $3\frac{1}{8}$ in/8 cm squares in the same way.

3 For the plain alternate squares, cut 5 in/12.5 cm strips and cross-cut into 5 in/12.5 cm squares. You will need 49 squares.

NOTE You may wish to delay cutting the plain alternate blocks (step 3) until you have pieced the pinwheel blocks. Seam allowance and stitching accuracy varies and you may find that your completed blocks are slightly more or slightly less than 5 in/12.5 cm. The alternate blocks must be exactly the same size as the pinwheel blocks if they are to fit together easily and well.

4 From the border fabric, if it is 60 in/154 cm wide, cut four 5 in/12.5 cm strips; if 45 in/115 cm wide, cut six strips of the same depth and set aside.

5 Cut the binding fabric into strips, $2\frac{1}{2}$ in/6 cm deep across the width of the fabric.

STITCHING

1 Draw a diagonal line across the wrong side of each of the 100 background squares with a marking pencil and ruler.

2 Take one pinwheel square and one background square and place right sides together. Stitch a seam line $\frac{1}{4}$ in/0.75 cm away from and on each side of the drawn diagonal line (diagram 1). Repeat with the remaining 99 squares. Use the chain piecing method to save time and thread.

diagram 1

3 Cut the threads between the squares. Press each stitched pair of squares flat to set the seams, then cut along the drawn diagonal line.

4 Press each unit open with the seam allowance towards the darker fabric. Trim off the small "ears" of fabric which extend beyond the square.

5 Lay out four squares as shown in diagram 2. You will see that pinwheel blocks are directional and can spin right or left depending how you place the units. Decide which way you want them to spin, then be consistent.

diagram 2

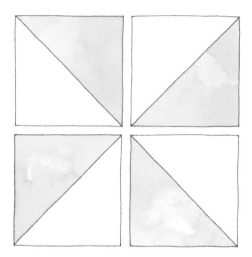

6 Pick up two of the units from the pinwheel and place one on top of the other, right sides together, carefully matching the edge you will stitch to join the units and making sure that the diagonal seams of both units butt together accurately. You can feel the fit with your fingertips. This is where careful attention to pressing always in the same direction really pays off.

7 Stitch along the righthand edge of the pair, then pick up the remaining pair of units from that pinwheel, snuggle the seam allowances together and stitch the seam. If you are not sure that you are stitching along the correct edge, pin the seam first and open out the pair, checking against your layout.

8 Chain piece all the remaining pinwheel units in pairs. Don't snip the thread between the pairs as you may find this little twist of thread will help to keep each pinwheel's pieces together (diagram 3).

diagram 3

9 Join each pair of half pinwheels to the other. Stitch along the long edge, taking particular care over the crossing point in the centre of the pinwheel (diagram 4). Press the seam open to reduce bulk in the centre of the block.

diagram 4

NOTE
It is worth taking time over matching points in the centre of the block but if you are not entirely happy with the end result you can sew a decorative button in the centre of the pinwheel (but not on quilts for babies or young children).

10 Lay the completed blocks on the floor, alternating with the plain squares, following the quilt assembly plan on page 184. Note that each even numbered row starts and finishes with a plain square, whereas the odd numbered rows begin and end with a pinwheel.

11 Pin and stitch the blocks into 11 rows, each containing 9 blocks, press the rows carefully. If you press the seam allowances between the blocks in opposite directions for alternate rows you will be able to butt them together when joining the rows, giving a neat fit with sharp points where the pinwheels meet.

12 Pin and stitch the rows together and press the top lightly.

ADDING THE BORDERS
1 Measure the patchwork top through the centre from top to bottom and cut both the side borders to this length. You may need to join strips to have pieces that are long enough. Pin and stitch to the sides of the patchwork. Press the seam allowance towards the borders.

2 Measure the patchwork top through the centre from side to side and cut both the top and bottom borders to this length. Pin and stitch to the top and bottom of the patchwork. Press as before.

FINISHING
1 Measure the completed patchwork top and if necessary cut and piece backing to fit with at least 2 in/5 cm extra on all sides. If you are joining the backing don't forget to cut off the selvages as these are very tightly woven and can cause distortion in the quilt. Press the seam open.

2 Spread the backing right side down on a flat surface, then smooth the wadding and the patchwork top, right side up, on top. Fasten together with safety pins or baste in a grid.

3 Mark the top with the desired quilting design. The quilt shown was marked in long diagonal lines through the plain squares and also through the diagonals of the pinwheels with a plastic tool called a Hera marker and a long ruler; the marker makes an indentation in the layered quilt which shows up well on light coloured fabric. Machine quilt along the marked lines.

4 Join the binding strips with diagonal seams to make a continuous length to fit all round the quilt and use to bind the edges with a double-fold binding, mitred at the corners.

Sherbet Twist

Designed by Sharon Chambers

Mouth-watering colours, a broderie anglaise frill and a scattering of mother-of-pearl buttons make this lap quilt the perfect treat for a sweet little girl. The plain white strips make assembly quick and easy and the quilt sandwich is simply secured with buttons.

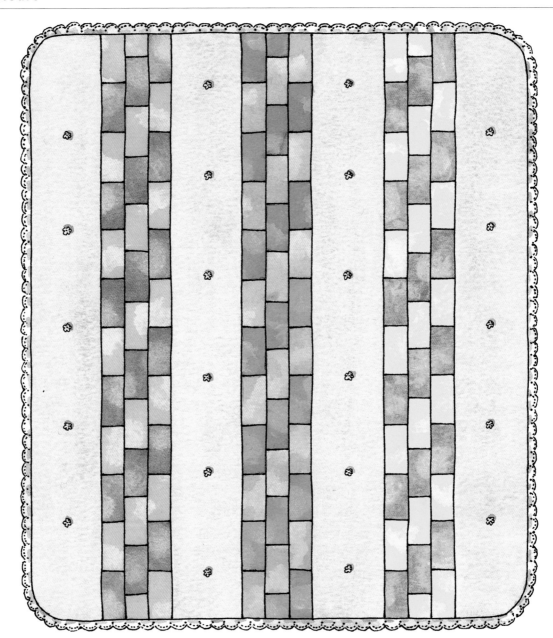

Finished size: 60 x 52½ in/144 x 126 cm

MATERIALS

All fabrics used in the quilt top are 45 in/115 cm
wide, 100% cotton.
The backing fabric is 60 in /150 cm wide.

For the sherbet twist strips: ⅓ yd/30 cm of each of
six different pastel colourways of the same fabric
design
Vertical sashing: white-on-white patterned fabric,
1¾ yds/1.6 m
Marking pencil
Pre-gathered broderie anglaise frill to edge quilt:
6½ yds/5.75 m

Buttons: 22 small mother-of-pearl
Backing: bleached calico, 1¾ yds/1.6 m
Wadding: soft 2 oz polyester, 56½ x 64 in/
136 x 154 cm
Quilting thread: white

NOTE

Because I wanted a puffy eiderdown
effect I used a double layer of 2 oz
wadding, which means two pieces of the
size given.

ALTERNATIVE COLOUR SCHEMES

The simplicity of this pattern allows for any favourite colour scheme a little girl could wish for: 1 Lilacs and pinks; 2 Minty greens with apricot; 3 Bright fruit sorbet combinations; 4 Lots of different floral prints.

1

2

3

4

diagram 1

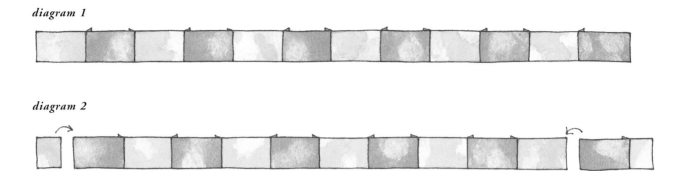

diagram 2

CUTTING

Before you cut your pastel fabrics, decide how to group them. There are three pairs of fabrics. Within each pair there is a dominant colour from which you will cut eighteen rectangles and a secondary fabric from which you will cut seventeen rectangles and two half rectangles.

1 From each of the pastel fabrics, cut three strips, 3 in/7.5 cm deep across the whole width of the fabric.

2 Divide your fabrics into your chosen pairs. From the dominant fabric of the first pair cross-cut the strips into 3 x 5½ in/7.5 x 13.5 cm rectangles. Each strip yields seven, but you only need eighteen. From your secondary fabric cross-cut two of the strips into 3 x 5½ in/7.5 x 13.5 cm rectangles to yield fourteen rectangles. From the third strip cut three more rectangles and two half rectangles 3 x 3 in/7.5 x 7.5 cm. Stack all of these in two piles and set aside.

3 Repeat step 2 for the other two pairs of pastels.

4 From the white-on-white patterned fabric, cut four strips, 8 in/19.5 cm wide down the length of the fabric, i.e. parallel to but not including the selvages.

STITCHING

1 Using your first pair of pastel fabrics, place one secondary fabric rectangle right sides together with a dominant fabric rectangle and stitch along a short side, taking a ¼ in/0.75 cm seam allowance. Continue in this fashion until you have seventeen pairs of rectangles stitched together.

2 Divide these into two stacks of six and one stack of five. Place the remaining rectangle and two half rectangles with the stack of five and set aside.

3 From the first stack of six, stitch the pairs together alternating the colours until you have a strip of twelve rectangles (diagram 1). Do the same for the second stack of six.

4 Stitch the last stack together into a strip of ten rectangles. Stitch one of the half rectangles to the remaining full-sized one, then add it to one end of the strip, keeping the alternate colours in their correct sequence (diagram 2). Add the remaining half rectangle to the other end of the strip.

5 Following the quilt assembly diagram on page 190, lay the three strips out so you can check that they are in the correct order. Press the seams towards the darker fabric. Pin and stitch the first and second strips together.

6 Add the third strip in the same way. Press the long seams towards the centre strip.

7 Stitch the second and third sets of fabric in the same way and press. You may find that there is a slight variation in length between the three sets of strips. If so, measure and trim them to the same length. Use this trimmed measurement to trim the four sashing strips to the correct size.

8 Pin one sashing strip to one pieced strip with right sides together and stitch with a ¼ in/0.75 cm seam allowance.

9 Pin and stitch the remaining four sashing strips in the same way. Press the seams towards the pieced strips.

ADDING THE FRILL

1 To round off the corners of the pieced top, use a saucer to mark the curve. Lay it on the corner so that the edge is just touching both sides, hold it firmly in place and draw around it with a marking pencil. Trim along the line (diagram 3). Repeat for all four corners.

diagram 3

2 To add the frill, start about three quarters of the way down on the righthand side and pin the broderie anglaise to the edge of the pieced top, right sides together, with the frill facing towards the centre of the quilt and the pre-gathered edge aligned with the edge of the quilt (diagram 4).

diagram 4

3 Overlap the end by about 1 in/2.5 cm. Unpin about 6 in/15 cm at the beginning of the frill and start stitching at that point taking a ¼ in /0.75 cm seam allowance. Stitch all around the quilt to about 6 in/15 cm from the end. Stop and break the thread.

4 Overlap the ends of the frill by about 1 in/2.5 cm and trim off the excess. Pin the short ends of the frill with right sides together. Stitch. Trim one side of the seam allowance to ¼ in/0.75 cm and fold the other side over it. Slip stitch the folded side down (diagram 5). Now that the ends are joined you can finish stitching the frill in place.

diagram 5

FINISHING

1 Trim your backing fabric to the same size as the quilt top.

2 If you are using 2 oz wadding doubled over, make sure that both layers are smooth. Lay the wadding on a flat surface. Place the backing fabric on the wadding right side up. Place the quilt on top with the right side down. Pin all three layers together, making sure that the frill is tucked inside so it doesn't get caught in the seam. Stitch around all four sides leaving an opening of about 15 in/40 cm on the bottom edge for turning. Turn the quilt right side out and slip stitch the opening closed behind the frill. Smooth the quilt out evenly and pin to hold it in place.

3 Hand-quilt "in-the-ditch" down the long seams. You will probably find that you have to take larger stitches because of the thicker wadding.

4 Finally, stitch the buttons in place using the quilt assembly diagram as a guide.

Tulip Field

Designed by Dorothy Wood

You can use any patterned fabric to make this quilt but to create a cohesive design choose plain fabrics in the exact shade of some of the colours in the pattern. Instead of quilting by hand or machine, the quilt is simply "tied" together at regular intervals with buttons. I chose rustic buttons that have a similar shade to one of the colours in the patterned fabric so that they contrast with the plain fabrics but still tone in with the quilt top as a whole.

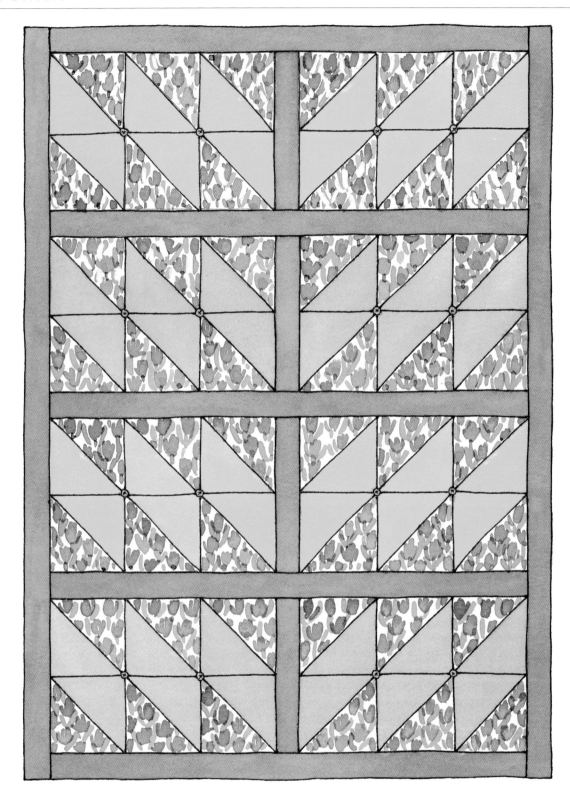

Finished size: 56 x 40 in /142 x 102 cm

MATERIALS

All fabrics used in the quilt top are 45 in/115 cm
wide, 100% cotton.
The backing fabric is 59 in /150 cm wide.

Tulip print: 1 yd/1 m

For the triangles: yellow and green, 18 in/50 cm

For the sashing and binding: pink, 1³⁄₄ yds/1.60 m

Backing: 40 x 56 in /102 x 142 cm

Wadding: low loft, 40 x 56 in/102 x 142 cm

White sewing thread

16 buttons

Deep pink sewing thread

Needle

ALTERNATIVE COLOUR SCHEMES

1 This bright flower fabric has a pale blue background colour that can be used for the binding and sashing – the paler colour softens the effect and pulls the fabrics together; 2 The classic blue and off-white combination will make a subtle country-style quilt ideal for a guest bedroom; 3 This striking fruit print will make a bright, bold quilt –use the yellow in the print as the alternative to the lime green in the blocks; 4 The paisley pattern combined with a spot fabric in matching colours gives a funky look for a young girl's bedroom.

1

2

3

4

CUTTING

NOTE Take care when cutting the tulip fabric so that you have the diagonal going in one direction for half the squares and in the other direction for the rest but the tulips still all point the same way.

1 From the tulip print, cut twenty-four 6⅞ in/ 17.5 cm squares ensuring that the tulips all face in the same direction. Cut 12 of the squares in half diagonally from top left to bottom right and the other 12 diagonally from top right to bottom left.

2 From both the yellow and the green fabrics, cut twelve 6⅞ in/17.5 cm squares. Cut each square in half diagonally.

3 From the pink fabric, cut four 12¼ x 2½ in/31 x 6.5 cm strips and three 37 x 2½ in/94 x 6.5 cm strips for the sashing; cut two 37 x 4½ in/94 x 11.5 cm strips and two 60 x 4½ in/152.5 x 11.5 cm strips, joining as necessary, for the binding.

STITCHING

1 Arrange the first block of yellow and tulip print triangles as shown in diagram 1. Stitch the triangles in pairs taking a ¼ in/0.75 cm seam allowance to make six squares. Press the seams towards the tulip print.

diagram 1

2 Stitch the top row of three squares together with ¼ in/0.75 cm seams and press the seams to the left. Stitch the bottom row of squares together and press the seams to the right.

3 Pin the two rows right sides together matching the seams. Stitch together with ¼ in/0.75 cm seams. Press the seam downwards.

4 Stitch the green and tulip print blocks in the same way, laying the triangles out as shown in diagram 2 to create the blocks before stitching so that no mistakes are made.

diagram 2

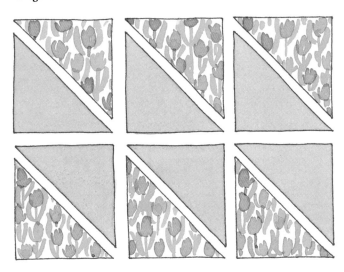

5 Repeat to stitch another block of yellow and tulip print squares and another of green and tulip print following the quilt assembly diagram on page 196, then reverse the layout of the triangles (following the quilt assembly diagram) and stitch two more blocks of yellow and tulip print plus two more of green and tulip print squares. Lay out the eight blocks as shown in the quilt assembly diagram.

6 Pin one of the short 12¼ x 2½ in/31 x 6.5 cm lengths of sashing right sides together along the right-hand side of the top lefthand yellow panel. Stitch with a ¼ in/0.75 cm seam and press away from the sashing. Pin the top righthand yellow panel to the other side of the sashing and stitch and press as before (diagram 3).

diagram 3

7 Stitch the two green panels together with a short strip of sashing in the same way, then the remaining panels. Press the seams towards the pieced blocks.

8 Fold the three middle-sized 37 x 2½ in/94 x 6.5 cm strips of sashing in half to find the mid point. Pin one strip along the bottom of the top yellow panel, right sides together and matching the mid point to the centre of the short sashing strip. Stitch with a ¼ in/0.75 cm seam.

9 Pin and stitch the first green panel to the other side of the sashing strip. Press the seams towards the blocks.

10 Work down the quilt adding sashing strips between the panels to create the pieced top as shown in the quilt assembly diagram.

11 Using ¼ in/0.75 cm seams, pin and stitch the two shorter binding strips across the top and bottom of the pieced top. Press the seams towards the blocks.

12 Pin and stitch the longer binding strips down each side of the pieced top. Press the seams towards the quilt.

FINISHING

1 Lay out the pieced top right side down. Place the wadding on top and smooth out, checking that there is the same amount of pink fabric border showing all round. Press the backing fabric and lay on top of the wadding right side up. Tack around the edge.

2 Fold under ¼ in/0.75 cm of the binding all round the pieced top and finger press to hold it in position. At the sides fold the binding over the wadding and backing fabric and pin. Fold over the binding along the top and bottom edges and pin.

3 Slip stitch the corners and hem the binding to the backing fabric (diagram 4). Turn the quilt over. Pin at the point between the coloured blocks where the buttons will be stitched.

diagram 4

4 Using a deep pink thread, sew a button where you have inserted the pins. Sew the threads to make a cross pattern on the button. Press the binding very gently to finish the quilt.

Matrix Quilt

Designed by Gail Smith

This quilt is very simple to make (it took approximately twelve hours) and with its contrasting sashing and borders, it's an ideal design to showcase your favourite fabrics. In this example, a collection of blue and green fabrics reminds us of the colours of the sea and it is framed perfectly by the dark blue sashing and borders.

Finished size: 62 x 42 in/155 x 107 cm

MATERIALS

All fabrics used in the quilt top are 45 in/115 cm wide, 100% cotton.

For centre squares and middle border: 6 in/15 cm across the width of at least 5 different blue and blue/green fabrics. These should be of approximately the same value, i.e. light or medium and preferably not too dark, as there needs to be a good contrast with the sashing fabric. (Fossil fern fabrics are ideal, also tone-on-tone fabrics.)

For middle border: 12 in/30 cm extra of one of the five fabrics above cut across the width

For inner and outer borders and the sashing: dark blue, 2¼ yds/2 m. This should be darker than the fabric for the squares.

Binding: 7½ in/19 cm, cut across the width. (We chose one of the fabrics used for the centre squares.)

Backing: size cotton or sheeting, 66 x 46 in/ 165 x 117 cm.

Wadding: either 2oz polyester or a cotton alternative, 66 x 46 in/165 x 117 cm

Machine thread: preferably cotton, to match

Variegated machine quilting thread (optional)

ALTERNATIVE COLOUR SCHEMES

1 Novelty fabrics for the centre square with dark sashing makes an equally bold design; 2 African fabric with coordinating sashing makes a great quilt for an animal lover; 3 Brown and gold fabrics give a classic look; 4 Pink and purple squares with toning lilac sashing produces a pretty, feminine design.

1

2

3

4

CUTTING

1 From the five strips for the centre squares, cut 40 squares measuring 6 x 6 in/15 x15 cm.

2 From the dark blue, cut four strips, 2 in/5 cm deep, across the width for the horizontal sashing strips.

3 From the remaining dark blue, cut eight strips, 2 in/5 cm wide and 54 in/137 cm long down the length of the fabric, four will be used for the vertical sashing and four for the inner borders; cut four strips, 2½ in/6 cm wide and 64 in/163 cm long down the length of the fabric for the outer borders.

4 From the middle border fabric, cut five strips, 1¼ in/3 cm deep across the width for the binding, totalling at least 200 in/508 cm altogether (to be joined together later).

5 Cut the binding fabric into strips, 1½ in/4 cm deep across the width of the fabric.

STITCHING

1 Lay out the 40 squares in five rows, each with eight squares across – the arrangement of the colours is not important at this stage. Place the four horizontal sashing strips in between.

2 To attach the sashing to the bottom of each square work as follows: lay a sashing strip right side up on your sewing machine, then place a 6 in/15 cm square, right side down on top of the sashing, aligning raw edges and stitch it to the sashing. Do not break the

thread or cut the sashing fabric but add another square right side down and stitch. Keep on going until you have attached seven squares in this way (diagram 1). You do not need to stitch on the remaining eighth square at this stage.

diagram 1

3 Repeat step 2 to attach the squares in the next four rows in the same way. You should have 5 spare squares.

4 Trim the sashing level with the squares and press the resulting units open with the seams pressed towards the sashing (diagram 2). Following the quilt assembly diagram on page 202, lay out the units in columns with the sashing strips at the bottom, varying the placing of the squares until you are happy with the layout. Take care not to have two squares the same colour close to each other and to balance the

diagram 2

colours across the whole quilt. Place a spare square at the bottom of each column. You may need to number them by pinning on strips of paper (column 1 unit 1, for example) to ensure they are stitched together in the same layout.

5 Starting at the top of column 1, stitch the sashing of unit 1 to the top of the square below it, and carry on down the first column. When you get to the bottom, attach the spare square. Repeat four times. You should now have five columns, each column starting and ending in a square. Press your work.

6 You are now ready to add the vertical sashing strips in between the rows. Taking your first column of units, pin one of the four vertical sashing strips (cut in step 3 of "cutting") to the righthand, long side, and stitch, being careful not to stretch the fabric. Press the seams towards the sashing (diagram 3). Repeat with three more rows, leaving one row over.

diagram 3

NOTE

Pin the columns together carefully and mark the position of the horizontal seams on the wrong side of the sashing before stitching, as the fabric can stretch and it is important to get the horizontal rows to line up as you stitch the vertical sashing strips in position. (They have a tendency to creep when being stitched together!)

7 Stitch the spare column of units to the righthand side of the patchwork panel.

ADDING THE BORDERS

1 Pin and stitch one of the four 2 in/5 cm inner border strips (cut in step 3 of "cutting") to one side of the patchwork top and repeat on the other side edge. Trim level, then add a strip to the top and bottom, press and trim.

2 For the middle border, measure the pieced top through the centre from side to side, then join strips to this measurement from the middle border fabric and stitch to the top of the patchwork. Repeat for the bottom strip.

3 Measure the pieced top through the centre from top to bottom, then join strips to this measurement from the middle border fabric and stitch to the side of the patchwork. Repeat for the other side.

4 Repeat the measuring and joining for the outer border and attach to all four sides of the quilt. Press your work.

FINISHING

1 Spread the backing right side down on a flat surface, then smooth the wadding and the patchwork top, right side up, on top. Fasten together with safety pins or baste in a grid.

2 Machine quilt with a straight stitch, using a walking foot and variegated thread, down each side of the sashing and one side of the outer border.

3 Join the binding strips cut in step 4 of "Cutting" with diagonal seams to make a continuous length to fit all round the quilt and use to bind the edges with a double-fold binding, mitred at the corners.

Red and White

Designed by Dorothy Wood

The two patterned fabrics used here are part of a range of matching fabrics that give the quilt a 1950s retro look. The circle pattern squares are cut on the straight grain so that the seams are easy to stitch and don't stretch out of shape. The wide binding is made by folding over the extra-large backing fabric, which is a quick and easy way of finishing off the edges.

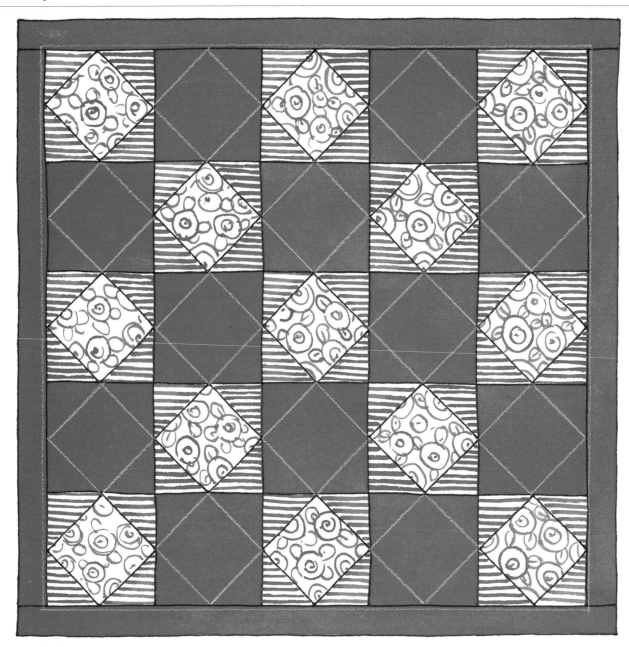

Finished size: 40 x 40 in/102 x 102 cm

MATERIALS

All fabrics used in the quilt top are 45 in/115 cm wide, 100% cotton.

The backing fabric used is 59 in/150 cm wide.

Red and white circle print: 12 in/30 cm
Red and white stripe: 20 in/51 cm
Solid red: 24 in/60 cm
Backing: red, 50 x 50 in/127 x 127 cm
Wadding: 40 x 40 in/102 x 102 cm
White sewing thread
Water soluble pen

ALTERNATIVE COLOUR SCHEMES

1 The matching stripe and check pattern fabrics make a subtle combination that can be softened with offwhite or brightened up with dark blue; 2 Choose baby pinks, blues and yellow to make a pretty cot quilt. Choose a baby print and pick out some solid colours to coordinate; 3 Contrasting fabrics made from the same print block are ideal for this quilt design. Choose one of the common colours for the whole squares; 4 Spot fabrics are always fun and often found in a range of different colourways that can be mixed and matched.

CUTTING

1 From the red and white circle print, cut two strips across the width, 6 in/15 cm deep, and cross-cut into thirteen 6 in/15 cm squares. Although they are set as diamonds on the quilt top, cut the squares on the straight grain.

> *NOTE*
>
> Take care when cutting the stripes that each square is exactly the same with the same width of stripe down each side. To make all the striped squares the same, you may need to cut off a narrow strip before cutting the next square.

2 From the red and white stripe, cut three or four strips across the width, $4\frac{3}{4}$ in/12 cm deep, then cross-cut into twenty-six $4\frac{3}{4}$ in/12 cm squares. Cut half the squares diagonally from top left to bottom right and the other half from top right to bottom left.

3 From the red fabric, cut three strips across the width, 8 in/20 cm deep, then cross-cut into twelve 8 in/20 cm squares.

STITCHING

1 Arrange the first block of red circle square and stripe triangles so that the stripes run vertically (diagram 1).

diagram 1

2 Lay one of the triangles face down on the square and pin so that an equal amount overhangs at each end. Stitch with a $\frac{1}{4}$ in/0.75 cm seam (diagram 2). Stitch the same triangle to all the red circle squares. Press the seams towards the stripe fabric.

diagram 2

3 Pin and stitch a triangle to the opposite side of each square. Press the seams towards the stripe fabric. Pin and stitch the remaining stripe triangles to the opposite sides of the squares, so that all the stripes are vertical. Press the seams towards the stripe fabric.

4 Following the quilt assembly diagram on page 208, arrange the patchwork blocks alternately with the solid red squares. Pin and stitch the blocks together in rows. Press the seams in adjacent rows in opposite directions.

5 Pin the rows together matching the seams carefully and stitch with a $\frac{1}{4}$ in/0.75 cm seam. Press the seams downwards.

ASSEMBLING

1 Place the backing fabric on a flat surface right side down and smooth out the wadding on top. Give the pieced top a final press and lay on top of the wadding right side up, so that there is a 5 in/13 cm border of backing fabric and approximately 3 in/7.5 cm of wadding all round. Fasten together with safety pins or baste in a grid.

2 Using the water soluble pen and a quilter's rule, draw lines between the red circle diamonds to mark a similar diamond on the red squares. On the red squares at the edge of the quilt, mark the centre point $\frac{1}{4}$ in/0.75 cm from the raw edge before completing the diamond (diagram 3).

diagram 3

3 Thread the machine with white thread. Stitch along the edge of the red circle squares and along all the marked lines in one direction. Turn the quilt and complete the stitching in the other direction. Bring all the thread ends to the right side. At the edge of the quilt the threads will be tucked behind the binding. Stitch any other thread ends into the quilt.

NOTE

When machine quilting, do not stitch beyond the edge on the diamonds at the edge of the quilt as the stitching will be visible on the reverse side.

4 Tuck the cutting mat between the wadding and the backing fabric down one side. Using the rotary cutter and quilter's rule, trim the wadding to 2 in/5 cm from the edge of the diamonds. Trim all edges the same.

5 Fold the red backing fabric over to the front level with the wadding and turn under the edge, so that it butts against the edge of the diamonds. Pin and tack (diagram 4). Fold over and tack the opposite side in the same way.

diagram 4

6 Fold in the two remaining sides to complete the binding. It may be easier to trim some of the excess fabric at the corners to reduce bulk. Slipstitch the corners only.

7 Machine stitch along the edge of the binding with white thread. Remove all tacking and press the binding lightly. Spray or sponge the quilt top with water to remove the marked lines and hang the quilt to dry.

Star Banner Wallhanging

Designed by Katharine Guerrier

Brighten a dark corner in the house with this vibrant wallhanging. The "Friendship Star" block is quick to make with speed piecing techniques and setting the blocks on a tilt gives them a contemporary look. An ingenious method of finishing the edges means that there is no binding, saving even more time. Small quilts like this can also be used to display a collection of brooches, badges or even a button collection.

Finished size: 39 x 15 in/99 x 38 cm

MATERIALS
All fabrics used in the patchwork top are
45 in/115 cm wide, 100 cotton.

Turquoise, blue and red: one fat quarter of each
Purple: 20 in/50 cm
Backing: 18 x 42 in/46 x 107 cm
Wadding: 18 x 42 in/46 x 107 cm
Tracing paper: one 8½ in/22 cm square
Flat-headed pins
Variegated machine embroidery thread for quilting

ALTERNATIVE COLOUR SCHEMES

1 Accentuate the star shapes with a bold fabric set in a neutral background;
2 Soft pastels make a pretty wallhanging for a guest bedroom; 3 Use novelty
fabrics to make a fun wallhanging; 4 These soft lilacs are a soothing combination for a bedroom wall.

1

2

3

4

CUTTING

1 From the four coloured fabrics cut $2\frac{7}{8}$ in/7.5 cm squares in the following quantities and colours:
eight red;
six blue;
eight turquoise;
six purple;
then cut $2\frac{1}{2}$ in/6.5 cm squares in the following quantities and colours:
four purple;
five turquoise;
five red;
one blue.

2 From the red, blue and turquoise, cut strips, $2\frac{1}{2}$ in/6.5 cm wide in the following lengths: two $6\frac{1}{2}$ in/16.5 cm and two $10\frac{1}{2}$ in/25.5 cm in each colour.

3 From the purple, cut four 4 in/10 cm strips for the borders in the following lengths: two 33 in/84 cm and two 16 in/40.5 cm. Cut one piece, 8 x 17 in/ 20 x 42 cm for the hanging sleeve.

STITCHING

1 Take one red and one purple $2\frac{7}{8}$ in/7.5 cm square and place right sides together. Draw a diagonal line on the reverse of the top square, then stitch down both sides of the line, $\frac{1}{4}$ in/0.75 cm away from it. Cut along the diagonal line and open out to make two half-square triangle units (see diagram 3, page 180). Repeat with the remaining $2\frac{7}{8}$ in/7.5 cm squares to make the following colour combinations and in the quantities given:
red/purple: four;
red/blue: eight;
blue/turquoise: four;
turquoise/purple: eight;
red/turquoise: four.

2 Now using four half-square triangle units and five squares for each block make three "Friendship Star" blocks as shown in diagram 1 and using the quilt assembly diagram on page 214 as a guide for the correct colour combinations and orientation of seams.

diagram 1

3 Using the $2\frac{1}{2}$ in/6.5 cm wide strips stitch borders around each of the blocks in the correct colour combinations (diagram 2). Press the seams towards the borders.

diagram 2

4 Cut a tracing paper template 8½ in/21.5 cm square. Lay this on each of the blocks in turn, setting the paper at a tilt. Attach the paper to the block with flat-headed pins and cut around the paper (diagram 3). Tilt the two blocks to the left and one to the right.

diagram 3

5 To make the sawtooth borders, stitch the remaining half-square triangle units into four strips of four squares in the following colour combinations: red/purple, red/blue, blue/turquoise and turquoise/purple (diagram 4). Press the seams towards the darker fabrics.

diagram 4

6 Following the quilt assembly diagram, stitch the sawtooth borders and blocks together taking the usual seam allowance.

ADDING THE BORDERS

1 Stitch the two longer purple 4 in/10 cm border strips to each side of the pieced top, then stitch the two shorter ones to the top and bottom, trimming the border strips to length if necessary. Shape the bottom of the quilt by drawing a line from the centre point of the bottom border to ½ in/1.5 cm below the seam line at both sides (diagram 5).

diagram 5

FINISHING

1 Cut the backing into two pieces across the width, then place these two pieces right sides together and stitch along one short edge taking a ¼ in/0.75 cm seam but leaving a 6 in/15 cm gap in the centre of the seam. Press the seam to one side.

2 Place the pieced top and the backing right sides together, smooth the two layers, then tack together. Trim the backing to the exact size of the quilt.

3 Place the wadding on a flat surface and lay the quilt and backing on top with the wrong side of the quilt against the wadding. Pin the layers together on the backing side.

4 With the backing on top and the wadding underneath, stitch all around the outer edges through all three layers with a walking foot and taking a ¼ in/0.75 cm seam allowance. Trim the wadding close to the stitching and clip the corners to reduce bulk.

5 Turn the quilt to the right side through the gap in the backing, this will bring the wadding between the quilt top and the backing. Finger press the seam flat so that it will lie along the outer edge of the quilt. Smooth the layers out from the centre and hold the layers together with a few pins.

6 Machine quilt using a walking foot. Using the variegated machine embroidery thread, outline the block seams and fill in the spaces with zig-zag lines. Outline the seams joining the sawtooth borders and the border seams (see page 18).

7 Make a hanging sleeve (see page 18) and attach.

Starry, Starry Lap Quilt

Designed by Rita Whitehorn

A cheerful lap quilt to warm up the winter evenings. The simple white patches in between the pieced blocks are embellished with star quilted patterns to echo the bright star fabric used in the border and strip patches.

Finished size: 57 x 46 in/ 141 x 117 cm

MATERIALS
All fabrics used in the patchwork top are
45 in/115 cm wide, 100% cotton.

For the stripes: ¼ yd/25 cm of three plain colours
(mauve, pink and green); ½ yd/50 cm of one cooler
colour (turquoise); 1 yd/85 cm of one stronger colour
(red)

Star fabric: 1¼ yds/1 m
White: ⅔ yd/60 cm
Backing: 2¾ yds/2.5 m
Wadding: 100% cotton, 60 x 50 in/130 x 155 cm
Template plastic
Marking pencil
Quilting threads: various colours to match the stripes

ALTERNATIVE COLOUR SCHEMES

In each of these different colourways the colours of the plain block have been picked out and repeated in the strips: 1 Choosing a striped fabric for the plain blocks makes a visually bold quilt; 2 Blues and aquas make a fresh, crisp colour combination for a country-style bedroom; 3 The clear blue print leads the way to a sunny colour scheme; 4 A glowing colour scheme based on the glittering insect print.

CUTTING

1 From each of the five colours for the stripes and from the star fabric, cut two strips, 2¼ in/5.5 cm deep across the width of the fabric.

2 From the white fabric, cut six squares, 10½ in/25.5 cm wide.

3 From the turquoise, cut four strips, 2½ in/6 cm deep across the width for the inner border.

4 From the red fabric, cut four strips 1½ in/4 cm deep across the width for the middle border. The remainder will be cut later for the binding.

5 From the star fabric, cut five strips, 5½ in/14 cm deep across the width for the outer border.

STITCHING

1 Lay out one of each of the 2¼ in/5.5 cm wide strips in your chosen sequence, then stitch together taking a ¼ in/0.75 cm seam allowance and press towards the darker fabrics (diagram 1).

diagram 1

2 Repeat step one above to make another block of stripes.

3 Sub-cut the above sections into six 10½ in/25.5 cm blocks (diagram 2).

diagram 2

4 Following the quilt assembly diagram on page 220, lay out the striped and white squares in three columns, four squares deep.

5 To assemble the first row, stitch a striped block to a white block, taking the usual seam allowance, then stitch another striped block to the other side of the white block. Press the seams towards the striped blocks.

6 To assemble the second row, stitch a white block to a striped block, then stitch a second white block to the other side of the striped block.

7 Pin and stitch the first row to the second row, being careful to match seams (diagram 3).

diagram 3

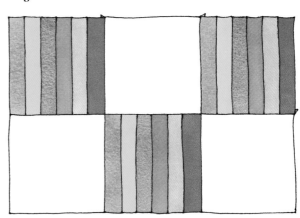

8 Stitch the third row as for the first and the fourth row as for the second. Pin and stitch these two rows together.

9 Finally, pin and stitch the unit made in step 7 to the unit made in step 8. Press the seams all in the same direction.

ADDING THE BORDERS

1 To make the inner border, stitch one turquoise 2½ in/6 cm strip to the top and one to the bottom of the pieced top, pressing seams towards the border. Trim the excess fabric, then stitch on the remaining turquoise strips to both sides and press as before.

2 To make the middle border, stitch one red 1½ in/4 cm strip to the top and one to the bottom of the pieced top, pressing seams towards the border. Trim the excess fabric, then stitch on the remaining red strips to both sides and press as before.

3 To make the outer border, stitch one 5½ in/14 cm star strip to the top and one to the bottom of the patchwork top, pressing seams towards the border. Trim the excess fabric. Cut one of the remaining star strips in two and join one half to each of the remaining two strips. Stitch to both side borders and press as before.

FINISHING

1 Make a star template from the template plastic in both of the sizes given opposite. Place these randomly on the white squares of the patchwork top and draw around the shape lightly with the marking pencil.

2 Cut the backing in half crosswise and stitch together down one long side. Press the seam open. Spread the backing right side down on a flat surface, then smooth the wadding and the pieced top, right side up, on top. Fasten together with safety pins or baste in a grid.

3 Hand quilt round the marked stars using different colours of quilting thread.

4 Machine or hand-quilt "in-the-ditch" between the middle and outer borders and between the stripes as shown in diagram 4.

diagram 4

Template

5 Trim off any excess wadding and backing fabric level with the pieced top.

6 Measure the quilt through the centre from top to bottom and cut two 2½ in/6 cm wide binding strips to this length, joining as necessary. Fold one binding strip in half lengthwise wrong sides together and pin to the side of the quilt, matching raw edges. Stitch approximately ½ in/1.5 cm in from the edge. Fold over to the back of the quilt and slip stitch down. Do the same on the opposite side of the quilt with the remaining strip.

7 Measure the quilt through the centre from side to side and add 1½ in/4 cm to this for turnings. Cut two more 2½ in/6 cm wide binding strips to this length, joining as necessary. Fold in half as before. Pin and stitch to the top and bottom of the quilt, turning in a short hem at either end before folding to the back.

Blue Ribbon Throw

Designed by Sharon Chambers

Impress your friends with the woven effect of blue ribbons in this intricate looking but simply pieced throw, backed with a sunny yellow. If you're hoping for a fast finish, this one's a sure bet and it can easily be made bigger for a bed quilt by adding more blocks.

Finished size: 54 x 42 in/140 x 105 cm

MATERIALS

All fabrics used in the quilt top are 45 in/115 cm
wide, 100% cotton.

For the background: blue and white all-over floral
patterned fabric, 1⅔ yds/1.5 m
For the ribbons: four contrasting blue fabrics, a long
¼ yd/25 cm of each
Backing: yellow, 1⅝ yds/1.5 m
Binding: dark blue, ⅝ yd/50 cm
Wadding: 46 x 58 in/115 x 150 cm
Machine quilting thread

NOTE

These fabrics need to be easily
distinguished from each other as well as from
the background. I chose a dark blue tone-on-
tone abstract, a medium/dark geometric, a medium blue and white check and a light/medium
small floral print, all of which look different from
each other and stand out well against the light
floral background.

ALTERNATIVE COLOUR SCHEMES

1 You could give this quilt a fresh look by putting the blue ribbons on a soft yellow background; 2 A pale peach background makes a very pretty colour combination; 3 A rose-coloured ground is also soft and cottagey; 4 For those who prefer a brighter look, try weaving the blue ribbons across a rich fuchsia abstract print.

CUTTING

1 From the floral patterned background fabric, cut eight strips, 6½ in/16.5 cm deep across the width of the fabric. Trim the selvages off. Cross-cut each strip into six squares 6½ x 6½ in/16.5 x 16.5 cm.

2 From one of the ribbon fabrics, cut one strip, 7½ in/19 cm deep, across the width of the fabric. Trim the selvages off. Starting at one end cross-cut the strip into twelve rectangles 1½ in/4 cm wide. Set these aside. Reduce the depth of the remaining strip, making it 6½ in/16.5 cm deep. From this cross-cut twelve more rectangles 1½ in/4 cm wide (diagram 1). Set aside.

diagram 1

3 Repeat step 2 for the remaining three ribbon fabrics.

4 From the binding fabric, cut six strips, 2½ in/6.5 cm deep, across the width of the fabric.

STITCHING

There are twelve blocks altogether. They are all the same pattern and they are all stitched exactly the same but with four different pairings of the ribbon fabrics. All seams are stitched with a ¼ in/0.75 cm seam allowance.

1 Study diagram 2 which shows the four block combinations and organize your strips to match. In Group A place the **short** medium blue and white check strips and the **long** medium/dark geometric strips. In Group B place the **short** medium/dark geometric strips and the **long** dark tone-on-tone strips. In Group C place the **short** light/medium small floral strips and

the **long** medium blue and white check strips. In Group D place the **short** dark tone-on-tone strips and the **long** light/medium small floral strips. You will be stitching all twelve blocks in one group at the same time, chain piecing for efficiency.

diagram 2

NOTE Stitching all of the blocks in a group at the same time saves confusion and means there is less risk of making a mistake.

2 Place twelve of the background squares and all of the strips from Group A next to your machine. With right sides together, stitch a short strip to one side of a centre square. Without breaking the thread stitch the second short strip and another square together. Continue until all twelve are stitched. Cut them apart and press all seams towards the short strip.

3 Stack all the partially-stitched blocks right side up next to your machine with the just-stitched strip at the top so that they are correctly aligned for adding the next strip. Stitch a long strip to the righthand side of the partially-stitched block and without breaking the thread do the same for the other eleven blocks in that group. Clip the threads and press the seams towards the long strip.

4 Repeat steps 2 and 3 for groups B, C and D. Pin an identifying letter to each finished stack if it helps to keep them organized.

5 Following diagram 2, lay out your stacks in similar positions. Stitch all of the A units to the Bs and all of the C units to the Ds (diagram 3). Press the seams towards the Bs and the Cs.

diagram 3

6 Pin and stitch the two halves together to make twelve larger blocks (diagram 4).

diagram 4

7 Following the quilt assembly diagram on page 226, lay out the blocks in sequence. Pin and stitch these together into four rows of three units each. Stitch the rows together. Make sure all the blocks stay in the correct alignment, and carefully match all seam lines, pinning as necessary. Press the last seams towards the bottom of the quilt.

FINISHING

1 Measure the pieced top and cut the wadding and the backing fabric at least 1 in/2.5 cm larger all around.

2 Spread the backing right side down on a flat surface, then smooth the wadding and the patchwork top, right side up, on top. Fasten together with safety pins.

3 Using a walking foot, machine quilt through all three layers along the seam lines.

4 Join the binding strips into one long length. Press in half wrong sides together down the entire length and use to bind the quilt with a double-fold binding, mitred at the corners.

Chenille Hearts

Designed by Sarah Wellfair

The chenille technique, also known as "slashing", is a great way to use up all those ugly fabrics from your stash – when they're used for the lower layers, they don't show but add to the felted edges when cut and washed. This technique makes quite a heavy quilt as it's made up of four layers but it is very soft and cozy.

Finished size: 37¾ x 34½ in/96.5 x 85.5 cm

MATERIALS

All fabrics used in the quilt top are 45 in/115 cm wide, 100% cotton.

Layers: plain purple, 2⅛ yds/2 m and bright pink, 1⅓ yds/1 m

Background: patterned purple, 1⅓ yds/1 m

Hearts: yellow and green, 10 in/25 cm of each

Backing: dark purple, 1⅓ yds/1 m

Lightweight card or plastic for template (optional)

Spray basting glue

Long ruler and marking pencil

Machine sewing cotton: 3 reels of thread to match backing

Chenille or slash cutter or sharp embroidery scissors

Binding: yellow, 12 in/30 cm

ALTERNATIVE COLOUR SCHEMES

1 The use of the batik stripe as the background fabric will give a bright orange in the slashes contrasting with the blue and green hearts; 2 This range of Christmas fabrics on a cream and gold background will make a striking festive throw; 3 This design just uses two colourways from the same fabric design creating a subtle contrast; 4 Setting the bright colours of the hearts against a calico background will really accentuate the heart motif.

1

2

3

4

CUTTING

1 From the plain purple, cut two pieces, 37 x 42 in/94 x 106.5 cm and from the pink layer fabric, cut one piece to the same size.

2 Cut the purple patterned background fabric to the same size as the plain fabrics.

3 Enlarge the heart motif opposite, then cut out the shape in card or plastic and use to cut four hearts out of each of the three bright fabrics (pink, yellow and green), making sure they are on the straight grain.

STITCHING

1 Press the dark purple backing and lay right sides down on the work surface.

2 Lay the three plain fabric pieces right sides up with the pink in the middle, then lay the purple patterned background fabric on top, right side up, and baste in place.

3 Place the four fabric sandwich on top of the backing fabric. These should be at least 1 in/2.5 cm smaller all round than the backing. Spray glue baste or tack these in place. Your stack of fabrics should be five deep (diagram 1).

diagram 1

4 Following diagram 2 below for positioning, spray glue baste or tack the hearts on top of the patterned purple, making sure they are on the straight grain.

5 Using a long ruler and pencil draw a line across the quilt at a 45 degree angle, starting in the bottom righthand corner – this is your first stitching line.

6 It is a good idea to stitch using a walking foot if you have one. Stitch on the line. Then, without breaking the thread, turn the quilt and stitch another line exactly parallel to the first, $\frac{1}{4}$ in/0.75 cm away from it. Repeat at the other end and continue until you reach the edge of the quilt (diagram 2). Turn the quilt and stitch the remaining half in the same way, so that the quilt is now covered with a grid of diagonal stitched lines.

diagram 2

7 Using sharp embroidery scissors, cut the top four fabrics between the diagonal lines of stitching for 1 in/2.5 cm, being careful not to cut the backing fabric. Do this at the start of every channel between the stitched lines. This will help when slashing (diagram 3).

diagram 3

8 Using your slash cutter or very sharp scissors insert between the rows of stitching on the sides you have just cut and carefully slash the fabric all the way along the channels, again being careful not to cut the backing. Slash all the channels. Take out any tacking.

9 Now that you have slashed your fabric, you will need to wash it in the machine to make the chenille bloom and fluff. A 40 degree wash is usually suitable for most fabrics. Tumble dry the quilt if possible.

10 Because you have stitched and cut on the bias your work may be a little out of shape after washing. Square up using a rotary cutter and cutting mat, trimming off the excess backing fabric at the same time.

11 Measure the quilt through the centre from top to bottom and cut two 3 in/7.5 cm wide binding strips to this length. Fold one binding strip in half lengthwise wrong sides together and pin to the side of the

Template
Enlarge by 200%

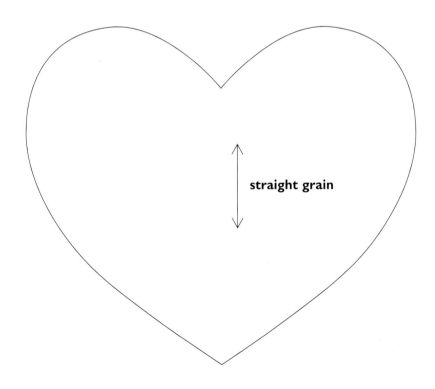

straight grain

quilt, matching raw edges. Stitch approximately ½ in/1.5 cm in from the edge. Fold over to the back of the quilt and slip stitch down. Do the same on the opposite side of the quilt with the remaining strip.

12 Measure the quilt through the centre from side to side and add 1½ in/4 cm to this for turnings. Cut two more 3 in/7.5 cm wide binding strips to this length. Stitch to the top and bottom of the quilt as before, turning in a short hem at either end before folding to the back.

NOTE A chenille quilt does not need to be quilted.

SUPPLIERS

UK

Abigail Crafts
3-5 Regent Street
Stonehouse
Gloucestershire GL10 2AA
Tel: 01453 823691
www.abigailcrafts.co.uk
Extensive range of patchwork and
embroidery supplies

The Bramble Patch
West Street
Weedon
Northants NN7 4QU
Tel: 01327 342212
Extensive range of patchwork and
quilting supplies

The Cotton Patch
1285 Stratford Road
Hall Green
Birmingham B28 9AJ
Tel: 0121 702 2840
Extensive range of patchwork and
quilting supplies

Creative Quilting
3 Bridge Road
East Molesey
Surrey KT8 9EU
Tel: 020 8941 7075
Specialist retailer

Custom Quilting Limited
"Beal na Tra"
Derrymihan West
Castletownbere
Co Cork
Eire
Email: patches@iol.ie
Long arm quilting services

Goose Chase Quilting
65 Great Norwood Street
Leckhampton
Cheltenham GL50 2BQ
Tel: 01242 512639
Patchwork and quilting supplies

Hab-bits
Unit 9, Vale Business Park
Cowbridge
Vale of Glamorgan CF71 7PF
Tel: 01446 775150
Haberdashery supplies

Patchwork Direct
c/o Heirs & Graces
King Street
Bakewell
Derbyshire DE45 1DZ
Tel: 01629 815873
www.patchworkdirect.com
Patchwork and quilting supplies and
accessories

Piecemakers
13 Manor Green Road
Epsom
Surrey KT19 8RA
Tel: 01372 743161
Specialist retailer and runs
workshops

Purely Patchwork
23 High Street
Linlithgow
West Lothian EH49 7AB
Scotland
Tel: 01506 846200
Patchwork and quilting supplies

The Quilt Loft
9/10 Havercroft Buildings
North Street
Worthing
West Sussex BN11 1DY
Tel: 01903 233771
Quilt supplies, classes and work-
shops

The Quilt Room
20 West Street
Dorking
Surrey RH4 1BL
Tel: 01306 740739
www.quiltroom.co.uk
Quilt supplies, classes and
workshops

Mail order:
The Quilt Room
c/o Carvilles
Station Road
Dorking
Surrey RH4 1XH
Tel: 01306 877307

Quilting Solutions
Firethorn
Rattlesden Road
Drinkstone
Bury St Edmunds
Suffolk IP30 9TL
Tel: 01449 735280
Email: firethorn@lineone.net
www.quiltingsolutions.co.uk
Long arm quilting services

Stitch in Time
293 Sandycombe Road
Kew
Surrey TW9 3LU
Tel: 020 8948 8462
www.stitchintimeuk.com
Specialist quilting retailer

Strawberry Fayre
Chagford
Devon TQ13 8EN
Tel: 01647 433250
Mail-order supplier of fabrics and
quilts

Sunflower Fabrics
157-159 Castle Road
Bedford MK40 3RS
Tel: 01234 273819
www.sunflowerfabrics.com
Quilting supplies

SOUTH AFRICA

Crafty Supplies
Stadium on Main
Main Road
Claremont 7700
Tel: 021 671 0286

Fern Gully
46 3rd Street
Linden 2195
Tel: 011 782 7941

Nimble Fingers
Shop 222
Kloof Village Mall
Village Road
Kloof 3610
Tel: 031 764 6283

Pied Piper
69 1st Avenue
Newton Park
Port Elizabeth 6001
Tel: 041 365 1616

Quilt Talk
40 Victoria Street
George 6530
Tel: 044 873 2947

Quilt Tech
9 Louanna Avenue
Kloofendal
Extension 5 1709
Tel: 011 679 4386

Quilting Supplies
42 Nellnapius Drive
Irene 0062
Tel: 012 667 2223

Simply Stitches
2 Topaz Street
Albernarle
Germiston 1401
Tel: 011 902 6997

Stitch 'n' Stuff
140 Lansdowne Road
Claremont 7700
Tel: 021 674 4059

AUSTRALIA

Country Patchwork Cottage
10/86 Erindale Road
Balcatta
WA 6021
Tel: (08) 9345 3550

Patchwork of Essendon
96 Fletcher Street
Essendon
VIC 3040
Tel: (03) 9372 0793

Patchwork Plus
Shop 81
7-15 Jackson Avenue
Miranda
NSW 2228
Tel: (02) 9540 278

The Quilters Store
22 Shaw Street
Auchenflower
QLD 4066
Tel: (07) 3870 0408

Quilts and Threads
827 Lower North East Road
Dernancourt
SA 5075
Tel: (08) 8365 6711

Riverlea Cottage Quilts
Shop 4, 330 Unley Road
Hyde Park
SA 5061
Tel: (08) 8373 0653

NEW ZEALAND

**Grandmothers Garden Patchwork
and Quilting**
1042 Gordonton Road
Gordonton
Hamilton
Tel: (07) 824 3050

Hands Ashford Craft Supply Store
5 Normans Road
Christchurch
Tel: (03) 355 9099
www.hands.co.nz

Needlecraft Distributors
600 Main Street
Palmerston North
Tel: (06) 356 4793
Fax: (06) 355 4594

Patchwork Barn
132 Hinemoa Street
Birkenhead
Auckland
Tel: (09) 480 5401

The Patchwork Shop
356 Grey Street
Hamilton
Tel: (07) 856 6365

The Quilt Shop
35 Pearn Place
Northcote Shopping Centre
Auckland
Tel: (09) 480 0028
Fax: (09) 480 0380

Spotlight Stores
Whangarei (09) 430 7220
Wairau Park (09) 444 0220
Henderson (09) 836 0888
Panmure (09) 527 0915
Manukau City (09) 263 6760
Hamilton (07) 839 1793
Rotorua (07) 343 6901
New Plymouth (06) 757 3575
Gisborne (06) 863 0037
Hastings (06) 878 5223
Palmerston North (06) 357 6833
Porirua (04) 238 4055
Wellington (04) 472 5600
Christchurch (03) 377 6121
Dunedin (03) 477 1478
www.spotlight.net.nz

Stitch and Craft
32 East Tamaki Road
Papatoetoe
Auckland
Tel: (09) 278 1351
Fax: (09) 278 1356

Stitches
351 Colombo Street
Christchurch
Tel: (03) 379 1868
Fax: (03) 377 2347
www.stitches.co.nz

Variety Handcrafts
106 Princes Street
Dunedin
Tel: (03) 474 1088